JIM
CORBET
Jungle Lore

JIM CORBETT

Jungle Lore

With an Introduction by
MARTIN BOOTH

OXFORD
UNIVERSITY PRESS

OXFORD
UNIVERSITY PRESS

YMCA Library Building, Jai Singh Road, New Delhi 110 001

Oxford University Press is a department of the University of Oxford. It furthers the
University's objective of excellence in research, scholarship, and education
by publishing worldwide in

Oxford   New York

Auckland Cape Town Dar es Salaam Hong Kong Karachi Kuala Lumpur
Madrid   Melbourne Mexico City Nairobi New Delhi Shanghai Taipei Toronto

With offices in

Argentina Austria Brazil Chile Czech Republic France Greece Guatemala
Hungary Italy Japan Poland Portugal Singapore South Korea Switzerland
Thailand Turkey Ukraine Vietnam

Oxford is a registered trademark of Oxford University Press
in the UK and in certain other countries

Published in India by Oxford University Press, New Delhi

First published 1990
Oxford India Paperbacks 1999
Fourteenth impression 2009

ISBN-13: 978-0-19-565185-0
ISBN-10: 0-19-565185-5

Typeset by Eleven Arts, Keshav Puram, Delhi 110 035
Printed in India by De Unique, New Delhi 110 018
Published by Oxford University Press
YMCA Library Building, Jai Singh Road, New Delhi 110 001

To Maggie

Contents

Introduction

IN THE SPRING OF 1985, I was sitting in a courtyard in Kaladhungi, Jim Corbett's village tucked against the first of the Himalayan foothills to rise from plains: around me was strewn the paraphernalia of the movie world. I was there for the filming of a drama documentary I had researched and written on the life of Jim Corbett, the culmination of years of keen ambition and a love and admiration for a man I never knew but who had, through his writings, fundamentally shaped my personal philosophy and attitude towards the natural world.

It was a fearfully hot day, even though early in the summer, and the film crew were hard at work arranging another set, in a local person's house, for the scene of Kunwar Singh's illness and Jim's saving of him from his opium addiction. Those not engaged in this work were squatting in the short shadows of late morning. I was with

Frederick Treves, the actor playing Jim Corbett—and who looks remarkably like him, more so in costume and make-up—resting under the scant shade of some paw-paw trees, when one of the local staff on the film crew came up to us.

'Sir,' he announced to me, 'there is an old fellow come who wants to meet Carpet Sahib.' He pronounced Corbett as 'Carpet' as was the way in the Kumaon district.

I supposed the old fellow wanted to meet the actor—others had done so before him, drawn by the magnetism of the 'glamourous' movies—and so asked Freddie Treves if this would be in order. He, with the good grace of the generous man he is, agreed, although I know actors shun such public contact.

An incredibly old man appeared. He must have been in his eighties, wizen and bent almost double by age. He walked with a stick newly cut from a tree and weeping sticky sap. As soon as he saw Freddie, he bowed low and sought to press his forehead to the actor's feet.

I said to the crew member, foolishly assuming the old man to be perhaps a little senile, 'I think you'd better tell him this is only an actor.'

This information was translated and a gabble of Kumaoni dialect made in reply.

'I have told the old fellow,' the crewman reported, 'that this is an actor from England, but he refuses to believe this. It is, he says, a legend that Carpet Sahib will return one day and he believes this is the true Sahib come back.' Then, with obvious reverential astonishment, for the crewman was a city dweller from New Delhi, he added, 'This old fellow has walked one hundred kilometres to see Carpet Sahib. *In just two days...*'

Anyone who has seen the Kumaon foothills will know that twenty kilometres would be a feat for an average fit man yet this old sage had walked virtually non-stop for forty-eight hours on hearing over the jungle grapevine that Corbett was returned to his home. It was Carpet Sahib's magnetism, still vibrant over the forty years since his departure from India, which had drawn the old man and not the spurious trappings of movies and modernity. This is the reverence with which the Kumaoni people viewed Corbett, and still do. It is the veneration afforded to a *sadhu*, a saintly man who has earned his reputation by example: in Corbett's case, by the example he set in the jungles of northern India.

Corbett's famous stories of man-eating tigers and leopard hunting make such exciting reading one tends to overlook in them, in the heat of the chase retold with such simplicity of style and immediacy of effect, the minutiae of detail appertaining to the hunter's skill. And, sadly, his man-eater books tend to overshadow his other volumes, *My India* and *Jungle Lore*. In these are shown, to an even greater extent, not only the hunter but also the man Corbett was.

The former volume deals, as every Corbett reader knows, with the author's familiarity with and love of India, his home for all but the last eight years of his very long life. Here is revealed his immense knowledge of India in all her variety: although he never travelled to the south of the subcontinent, he knew the north and centre well. Yet it is in this book, *Jungle Lore*, that one sees the real soul of Corbett, the core of his love affair with the land of his birth—the jungles of the north and the people (in his mind, both human and animal folk) who inhabit it.

Jungle Lore is probably the least known of Corbett's books. It does not contain sustained anecdotes of hunting dangerous cats or in-depth stories of jungle or forest encounters. Instead, it deals quite simply—occasionally almost naïvely—with the close relationship between Corbett and the natural world and the immense value such an intimacy bears for all men. It is also the nearest he came to an autobiography.

Much of Corbett's childhood, as regards his experiences in the jungle, is here—his early forays with catapult and bow-and-arrow, his first gun and first adventures: but these are not presented as thrilling episodes (although they are) but as lessons attended in the jungle's classroom. For Corbett, term-time at the jungle school never ended and he never graduated, for it is impossible ever to do so: there is always more to learn, more to discover and more to observe because the jungle and the world of nature is in permanent flux.

The crux of *Jungle Lore*, however, is not restricted to learning and seeing. It is more to do with feeling, with sensibility and sensitivity—and it is here that Corbett stakes his claim to fame and posterity—and with presenting nature's case to a world fast ignoring the wonders of the animal (and plant) kingdoms. For, in *Jungle Lore*, written thirty-seven years ago, Jim Corbett is lamenting the divorce of modern man from his environment. He learns the lessons and, like all good teachers, he seeks to share his knowledge and the implications of it with others.

This book has not dated with the passing years. Its import is as vibrant today as ever it was, the morality even more seminal. Sadly, the morals Corbett espouses are still blatantly ignored. Much of Corbett's jungle has gone: the Siwalik Hills which he roamed are mostly denuded of trees, ravaged by erosion and mostly devoid of tigers and game. He would not recognize his Kumaon homeland now.

Yet pockets do remain. The reader can still wander a little way down the wooded firetrack to Powalgarh, still sit on the Boar River bridge, still see the wall Corbett and the villagers built around their fields to keep the wild pigs out of the crops—though the absence of these creatures has long since rendered that defence redundant.

Jungle Lore has a poignant and very pertinent message. It begs us to stop the disaster of raping the earth mother, entreats us to re-assert and re-affirm our contacts with the natural world, to get to know, understand and use to a mutual advantage the ways—the lore—of the wild.

MARTIN BOOTH

chapter one

FOURTEEN OF US—BOYS AND girls ranging
in age from eight to eighteen—were sitting on
the wing wall of the old wooden cantilever bridge
over the Boar river at Kaladhungi, listening to
Dansay telling ghost stories. The bonfire we had
made in the middle of the road, from brushwood collected in the nearby jungle, had burnt
down to a red glow and with darkness closing
down Dansay had selected just the right time
and setting for his stories, as was evident from
the urgent admonition of one of the nervous
girls to her companion: 'Oh *don't* keep looking
behind. You *do* make me feel so nervous.'

Dansay was an Irishman steeped to the
crown of his head in every form of
superstition, in which he had utter and
complete belief, and it was therefore
natural for him to tell his ghost stories
in a very convincing manner. The

stories he was telling that night related to shrouded figures and rattling bones, the mysterious opening and closing of doors, and the creaking of boards on stairways in old ancestral halls. As there was no possibility of my ever seeing a haunted ancestral hall, Dansay's ghost stories held no terrors for me. He had just finished telling his most blood-curdling story and the nervous girl had again admonished her companion not to look behind, when the old horned fish owl who spent all his days dozing on the dead branch of a tree roofed over with creepers—where he was safe from the attention of crows and other birds that love to bait owls—started on his nightly quest for fish and frogs in the Boar river by giving vent to his deep-throated call of *Ho Har Ho* from the topmost branch of the *haldu* tree that had been blasted by lightning and that was a landmark to those of us who, armed with catapult or butterfly net, ventured into the dense jungle in which it stood. The call of the owl, often mistaken by the ignorant for the call of a tiger, was answered by his mate who, except in the mating season, lived in a *pipal* tree on the bank of the canal, and was an excuse for Dansay to end his ghost stories and switch over to stories about banshees, which to him were even more real and more to be feared than ghosts. According to Dansay a banshee was an evil female spirit that resided in dense forests and was so malignant that the mere hearing of it brought calamity to the hearer and his family, and the seeing of it death to the unfortunate beholder. Dansay described the call of a banshee as a long drawn-out scream, which was heard most frequently on dark and stormy nights. These banshee stories had a fearful fascination for me, for they had their setting in the jungles in which I loved to roam in search of birds and their eggs and butterflies.

I do not know what form the banshees took that Dansay heard in Ireland, but I know what form two of them took that he heard in the jungles at Kaladhungi. About one of these banshees I will tell you later, the other is known to all the people who live along the foothills of the Himalayas, and in many other parts of India, as a *churail*. The *churail*, the most feared of all evil spirits, appears in the form of a woman. Having cast her eyes on a human being this woman, whose feet are turned the wrong way, mesmerizes her victims, as a snake does a bird, and walking backwards lures them to their doom. When danger of seeing the woman threatens, the only defence against her wiles is to shield the eyes with the hands, any piece of cloth that is handy, or, if indoors, to pull a blanket over the head.

Whatever the human race may have been in the days of the cave man, we of the present day are essentially children of the daylight. In daylight we are in our element and the most timid among us can, if the necessity arises, summon the courage needed to face any situation, and we can even laugh and make light of the things that a few hours previously made our skin creep. When daylight fades and night engulfs us the sense of sight we depended on no longer sustains us and we are at the mercy of our imagination. Imagination at the best of times can play strange tricks, and when to imagination is added a firm belief in the supernatural it is not surprising that people surrounded by dense forests, whose only means of transport is their own feet, and whose field of vision at night is limited to the illumination provided by a pine torch, or a hand lantern when paraffin is available, should dread the hours of darkness.

Living among the people and for months on end speaking only their language, it was natural for Dansay to have superimposed their superstitions on his own. Our hillmen do not lack courage, and Dansay was as brave as man could be; but because of their belief in the supernatural, I am convinced that neither the hillmen nor Dansay ever dreamed of investigating what the former called a *churail* and the latter believed was a banshee.

During all the years I have lived in Kumaon, and the many hundreds of nights I have spent in the jungles, I have heard the *churail* only three times—always at night—and I have seen it only once.

It was the month of March. A bumper mustard crop had just been harvested, and the village in the midst of which our cottage is situated was alive with happy sounds. Men and women were singing and children were calling to each other. The moon was a night or two from the full, and visibility was nearly as good as in daylight. Maggie and I were on the point of calling for dinner—the time was close on 8 p.m.—when clear and piercing on the night air came the call of the *churail*, and instantly every sound in the village was hushed. In the right-hand corner of the compound, and some fifty yards from our cottage, stands an old *haldu* tree. Generations of vultures, eagles, hawks, kites, crows, and glossy ibis, have worn the bark off and killed the upper branches of the old tree. Opening our front door, which had been closed against the cold wind blowing down from the north, Maggie and I stepped out on to the veranda, and as we did so, the *churail* called again. The call came from the *haldu* tree and there, sitting on the topmost branch in brilliant moonlight was the maker of the call, the *churail*.

It is possible to describe some sounds by a combination of

letters or of words, as for instance the 'cooee' of a human being, or the 'tap, tap, tapping' of a woodpecker, but no words of mine can describe the call of the *churail*. If I said it resembled the cry of a soul in torment, or of a human being in agony, it would convey no meaning to you, for neither you nor I have heard either of these sounds. Nor can I liken the call to any other sounds heard in the jungles, for it is something apart, something that does not appear to have any connexion with our world and that has the effect of curdling the hearer's blood and arresting his heart-beats. On the previous occasions on which I had heard the call I knew it emanated from a bird and I suspected the bird to be an owl, possibly a migrant, for I know every bird in Kumaon and its call, and this was no bird of our jungles. Stepping back into the room I returned with a pair of field-glasses which had been used during the Kaiser's war for spotting for artillery and which were therefore as good as glasses could be. With these I examined the bird very carefully. I will describe what I saw in the hope that someone, more knowledgeable than myself, will be able to identify it.

(a) In size the bird was a little smaller than a golden eagle.

(b) It stood upright on its rather long legs.

(c) Its tail was short, but not as short as an owl's tail.

(d) Its head was not round and big like the head of an owl, nor did it have a short neck.

(e) On its head there was no crest or 'horns'.

(f) When it called—which it did at regular intervals of about half a minute—it put its head up facing the heavens, and opened its beak wide.

(g) In colour it was an overall black, or possibly a dark brown which looked black by moonlight.

I had a 28-bore shot gun, and a light rifle in the gun rack. The gun was useless, for the bird was out of range of it, and I was frightened to use the rifle. Accuracy of aim cannot be depended on in moonlight, and if I missed the bird everyone within hearing distance would be more convinced than ever that the call was being made by an evil spirit which even a rifle bullet was of no avail. After calling about twenty times the bird spread its wings, and gliding off the tree, vanished into the night.

The village sounds were not resumed, and next day no references was made to the *churail*. 'When in the jungles,' warned my poacher friend Kunwar Singh when I was a small boy, 'never speak of a tiger by its name, for if you do, the tiger is sure to appear.' For the same reason the people of our foothills never talk of the *churail*.

The younger members of the two large families who spent the winter months in Kaladhungi numbered fourteen, excluding my younger brother who was too small to take part in the nightly bonfire or to bathe in the river, and who therefore did not count. Of these fourteen, seven were girls, ranging in age from nine to eighteen, and seven were boys, ranging in age from eight to eighteen, of whom I was the youngest. This handicap, of being the youngest of the males, saddled me with tasks that I disliked intensely, for we were living in the Victorian age and when, for instance, the girls went bathing in the canal that formed one boundary of our estate, which they did every day except Sunday— why girls should not bathe on Sunday I do not know—it was deemed necessary for them to be accompanied by a male whose age would offer no offence to Mother Grundy. The selected victim being myself, it was my duty to carry the towels and nightdresses of the girls— for there were no swim- suits in those days—and to keep guard while the girls were bathing and warn them of the approach of males, for there was a footpath on the opposite bank of the canal which was occasionally used by men on their way to collect firewood in the jungles, or to work on the canal when it needed repair or cleaning. The canal was a masonry one, ten feet wide and three feet deep, and where there was an inlet for irrigating our garden the King of Kumaon, General Sir Henry Ramsay, had had the bed of the canal scooped out for a few yards to a depth of six feet, and every day before I set out with the girls I was cautioned not to allow any of them to get drowned in this deep part. The entering of running water while wearing a thin cotton nightdress is a difficult feat, if the proprieties are to be maintained, for if the unwary step into three feet of water and sit down—as all girls appear to want to do the moment they get into the water—the nightdress rises up and flows over the head, to the consternation of all beholders. When this happened, as it very frequently did, I was under strict orders to look the other way.

While I was guarding the girls, and looking the other way when the necessity arose, the other boys armed with catapults and fishing-rods were making their way up the canal bank to the deep pool at the head of the canal, competing as they went as to who could shoot down the highest flower off the *samal* trees they passed, or put the first pellet into the ficus tree on the canal bank, a hit only being allowed when the milk-like sap— the best medium for the making of bird-lime—trickled down the bole of the tree. And there were birds to be fired at, hair-crested drongos, golden orioles, and rosy pastors that drink the nectar of the *samal* flowers; common, slaty, and rose-headed paroquets that nipped off the *samal* flowers and, after nibbling a small portion, dropped the flowers to the ground for deer and pigs to eat; crested pied kingfishers who when disturbed went skimming up the canal, and always the horned owl—the mate of the one who lived on the far side of the Boar bridge—whose perch was on a branch of the *pipal* tree overhanging the canal, and who had never been known to let anyone get within catapult range but who nevertheless was always fired at. Arrived at the big pool there would be fierce competition to see who could land the most fish on improvised tackle of thread borrowed from their respective mother's or sister's work baskets, bent pins for those who could not afford the regulation hook, and rods made from the side-shoots of bamboos. The fishing ended when the supply of paste, used as bait, was exhausted or had been dropped by a careless hand into the water, and with a catch of a few small *mahseer*—for our rivers were full of fish—clothes were hastily discarded and all lined up on the big rock overhanging the pool and, at a signal, dived off to see who could reach the far bank first. And while the others were indulging in these fascinating sports I, a mile lower down the canal, was being told to look the other way or being reprimanded for not having given warning of the approach of the old villager who had passed carrying a load of wood on his head. One advantage I derived from my enforced labour, it let me into all the secret plans the girls made for the playing of practical jokes on the boy members of the two families in general, and on Dansay and Neil Fleming in particular.

Dansay and Neil were both mad Irishmen, and here their similarity ended, for while Dansay was short, hairy, and as strong as a grizzly bear, Neil was tall and willowy and as fair as a lily. The difference even went deeper, for whereas Dansay would think nothing of shouldering his muzzle-loading rifle and stalking

and shooting tigers on foot, Neil had a horror of the jungles
and had never been known to fire a gun. One thing they had
in common, hatred of each other, for both were madly in love
with all the girls. Dansay—who had been disinherited by his
father, a General, for refusing to go into the Army—had been
at a Public School with my elder brothers and was at that time
resting between the job he had lost in the Forest Service and
the one he hoped some day to get in the Political Service. Neil
on the other hand was a working man, assistant to my brother
Tom in the Postal Service; and the fact that neither was in a
position to dream of matrimony in no way damped their affection
for the girls or lessened their jealousy of each other.

From conversations overheard on the canal bank I learned
that friend Neil on his last visit to Kaladhungi had been too full
of himself and was beginning to imagine things, whereas Dansay
on the other hand was too subdued and very slow in coming
forward. To rectify this unsatisfactory state of affairs it was
thought necessary to pull Neil down a whole row of pegs, and
elevate Dansay a little: 'Not too much, my dear, or he will then
begin to imagine things.' What 'imagining things' meant I did
not know, and I thought it best not to ask. To accomplish these
desired ends, with one stroke if possible, it would be necessary
to include both the too ardent Neil, and the too slow Dansay
in the same practical joke. Many plans were discussed and the
one eventually agreed on needed the co-operation of brother
Tom. Work during the winter months was not heavy in Naini
Tal and Tom was in the habit of allowing Neil to absent himself
every alternate week from Saturday evening to Monday morning.
This brief holiday Neil spent with one or other of the two families
in Kaladhungi, in both of which he was welcome for his genial
nature and his grand voice. Accordingly a letter was sent to Tom
asking him to detain Neil on one pretext or another on the

coming Saturday evening, and to send him off on his fifteen-mile walk to Kaladhungi so as to arrive at the end of his journey as night was falling. Further, Tom was to hint to Neil that the girls would probably get alarmed at his late arrival and would walk up the road to meet him. The plan that had been agreed on for this, the greatest of all practical jokes, was that Dansay, sewn up in one of his bear skins, was to be conducted by the girls two miles up the Naini Tal road to where there was a sharp bend on the road. At this point Dansay was to take up position behind a rock and, when Neil arrived, roar at him in a bear-like manner. Neil, on seeing the bear, was expected to dash down the road into the arms of the waiting girls who, on hearing his story, would pass uncomplimentary remarks on his bravery, and scream with laughter in which Dansay would join when he arrived on the scene a minute later. Dansay raised objections, which he withdrew when he was told that the strip of red flannel he had found in his ham sandwich, and which had caused him a lot of embarrassment at a picnic two weeks previously, had been inserted at Neil's suggestion.

Traffic on the Kaladhungi-Naini Tal road ceased at sundown and on the appointed evening Dansay, sewn into one of his bear skins, was led by the girls, at times on all fours and at times on his flat feet, to the pre-arranged spot where—the evening being warm and the skin having been sewn over his clothes—he arrived in a bath of sweat. In the meantime up in Naini Tal Neil was chafing at being given one job after another until the time had passed when he usually started on his walk to Kaladhungi. Eventually he was told that he could go, and before he left, Tom produced his shot gun and putting two cartridges into it placed it in Neil's hands and warned him that it was only to be used in emergency. The road from Naini Tal to Kaladhungi is downhill most of the way and for the first eight miles passes through patches of cultivation; thereafter, and right down to Kaladhungi, it runs through more or less dense forest. Dansay and the girls had been in their respective positions for some time, and the light was beginning to fade, when down the road came Neil singing 'Killarney' at the top of his voice, to keep his courage up. The singing came nearer and nearer—the girls said later that they had never heard Neil in better voice—and then round the bend where Dansay was waiting for him came Neil. Acting on instructions, Dansay stood up on his hind legs and roared at Neil in a bear-like manner, and Neil *threw up his gun and fired off both barrels.* A cloud of smoke obscured Neil's vision and as he started to run away he heard the 'bear' go rolling down the hill out of sight. At that moment the girls came running up the road, and at the sight of them, Neil brandished his gun and said he had just shot a huge bear that had made a furious attack upon him. Asked by the horrified girls what had become of the bear Neil pointed down the hill and invited the girls to accompany him to have a look at his bag, adding that it would be quite safe to do so for he had shot the bear dead. Declining the invitation the girls told Neil to go down alone and nothing loth Neil— who was greatly touched by the tears of the girls which he thought were being shed at his narrow escape from the bear—went down the hill. What Dansay said to Neil and what Neil said to Dansay is not on record; but when, after a long interval, they scrambled up to the road—where the girls were anxiously waiting—Dansay was carrying the gun, and Neil was carrying the bear's skin. Dansay, who in his roll down the steep hillside had been saved from injury by the bear's skin, asserted that Neil had shot him in the chest and knocked him off his feet. And when Neil explained how he came into possession of the gun, which had so nearly caused a fatal accident, the blame for the miscarriage of the whole enterprise was heaped on brother Tom's absent head.

Monday was a government holiday and when Tom arrived on Sunday night to spend the holiday at home, he was confronted by a bevy of angry girls who demanded to know what he meant by entrusting a man like Neil with a loaded gun and thereby endangering the life of Dansay. Tom listened while the storm broke over his head, and when the narrator got to the part where Dansay had been shot in the chest and knocked off his feet and the girls had wept in each others arms at his untimely death, Tom scandalized all present by bursting into peals of laughter, in which all but Dansay joined when he explained that suspecting—from the letter he had received—that mischief was on foot he had extracted the bullets from the cartridges, and loaded them with flour. So the net result of the great practical joke was not what had been expected, for Neil got more full of himself, while Dansay got more subdued.

chapter two

OWING TO MY ASSOCIATION WITH the girls
Dansay suspected me, quite wrongly, of having
had a hand in the bear incident out of which he
had not come with as much credit to himself as
had been expected, for the only contribution I
had made was to suggest that strong twine be
used to sew him into the bear's skin instead
of thread. To no other reason can I ascribe
his invitation to me one morning—while I was
showing my companions how to swing
from one branch of a tree to another—to
accompany him on a shoot. Uplifted to the
seventh heaven at having been selected for this
great honour I set out with Dansay who—
after we had started—said he would show me
how to shoot a tiger on foot. At the Dhunigar
canebrakes—the home of tigers as I found in
subsequent years—we saw many pug
marks but no tigers, and on the way

home Dansay, who was a friend of the family, decided to give
me my first lesson in firing a gun. At the time he came to this
decision we were standing at one end of an open glade, at the
other end of which a number of white-capped laughing thrushes
were turning up the dead leaves in search of white ants. While
we had been after the tigers Dansay had carried his muzzle-
loading rifle in his hands and his shotgun—also a muzzle-
loader—slung over his shoulder. He now unslung the shotgun
and placing it in my hands pointed to the thrushes and instructed
me to put my left foot a little in advance of the right, raise the
gun to my shoulder, hold it steady, and gently press the trigger,
all of which I did. Even after this long lapse of years I am not
sure in my mind whether the gun had been specially loaded
for my benefit or whether Dansay who, as I have told you, was
as strong as a grizzly bear, was in the habit of over-charging his
gun. Anyway, when I recovered sufficiently to pick myself up
and take an interest in my surroundings I saw Dansay running
his hands along the barrels of the gun to see if they had got
dented on the stones on to which I flung the gun as I went
heels over head on pressing the trigger. The thrushes had all
gone but on the ground on which they had been feeding we
found a white-browed flycatcher, a bird about the size of a robin.
On examining the little bird we found no signs of injury and
Dansay concluded it had died of shock, a conclusion with which
I was in entire agreement, for I too had nearly died of shock.

Shortly after my experience with Dansay's muzzle-loader my
eldest brother Tom who, on the death of my father when I was
four years of age, had taken over the responsibilities of the family,
announced one evening that he was going to take me out bear
shooting. The announcement was received with consternation
by my mother who, though she had the courage of Joan of Arc
and Nurse Cavell combined, was as gentle and as timid as a dove.

I listened interestedly while Tom—on whom I lavished all of a small boy's hero worship—assured my mother that there was no danger, that he would take great care of me, and that I would come to no harm. When my mother eventually gave her consent to my going bear shooting I determined I would keep out of harm's way by sticking to brother Tom's heels like glue.

We proceeded that evening—Tom carrying both his own rifle and a gun for me—along a game track that ran across the face of a great mountain. Half-way across the mountain we came to a deep, dark, and evil-looking ravine. Tom stopped at the edge of the ravine and whispered to me that it was a grand place for bears, who either went up or down the ravine or came along the game track. He then pointed to a rock on the side of the track for me to sit on, put the gun and two ball cartridges into my hands, and warned me to be very careful to kill and not wound any bears I fired at. Then, pointing to a solitary oak tree on the shoulder of the mountain eight hundred yards away, he said he was going there and that if during the course of the evening I saw a bear anywhere in his vicinity and in a position in which I thought he could not see it, I was to go and tell him, and with these parting words *Tom left me*.

A wind was blowing, rustling the dry grass and dead leaves, and my imagination filled the jungle round me with hungry bears. (During that winter nine bears were shot on that mountain.) That I would presently be eaten I had no doubt whatever, and I was quite sure the meal would prove a very painful one for me. Time dragged on leaden feet, each moment adding to my terror, and when the glow from the setting sun was bathing the mountain side in red, I saw a bear slowly making its way along the skyline a few hundred yards above Tom's tree. Whether Tom had seen the bear or not mattered no jot to me. The opportunity I had been praying for to get away from that terrifying spot had come, and I was going while the going was still good. So, shouldering the gun, which after my experience with Dansay's muzzle-loader I had been too frightened to load, I set off to tell Tom about the bear and to reattach myself to him.

The Himalayan black bear, in our part of the world, live throughout the winter on acorns. Bears are heavy and acorns grow at the extremities of oak branches, and in order to get at the acorns bears bend the branches inwards towards the centre of the tree. Some of these branches are only cracked and remain green for years, others are torn right off and fall to the ground when released, while others again are left dangling by a strand of bark. I had crossed the ravine and entered a dense patch of undergrowth when I heard a rushing sound. Petrified, I stood quite still while the sound grew louder and louder, and then with a crash a big object fell right in front of me. It was only a branch which a bear had left dangling on the tree under which I was passing, and which the wind had dislodged, but had it been the biggest bear in Asia it could not have frightened me more. The courage I had summoned to take me to brother Tom had all gone, so back to my rock I crept. If a human being in normal health can die of fear, I would have died that night and many times since.

The red glow had faded off the mountain and the light gone out of the sky, when a figure loomed out of the darkness and a cheery voice hailed me. 'You have not been feeling frightened, have you?' Tom asked as he took my gun, and when I said I was not feeling frightened *now*, Tom left it at that, for he was a wise and a very understanding brother.

Tom was a great believer in making an early start when he went shooting, and the morning he took me with him to shoot peafowl he roused me at 4 a.m., made me wash and dress as silently as possible in order not to disturb the rest of the family and, half an hour later, with a hot cup of tea and home-made biscuits to sustain us, we set out in the dark on our seven-mile walk to Garuppu.

In my lifetime I have seen great changes in the forests of the Tarai and Bhabar. Some of these changes have resulted from exploitation, others have been brought about in a natural manner. In some areas where there were dense virgin forests there is now scrub jungle, and where there were wide open stretches of grass and plum bushes there is now forest. To the south east of Garuppu where there is now tree jungle, there was (at the time I am writing about), waist-high grass and plum bushes. It was this area that Tom was making for on that December morning, for the plums were ripe and were an irresistible attraction, not only to deer and pigs but also to peafowl.

It was still dark when we arrived at Garuppu so we sat near the well while light gradually appeared in the east, listening to the jungle awakening. On all sides red jungle-cocks were crowing, arousing from their slumbers a multitude of smaller birds each of which, as it shook the dew from its feathers and the sleep out of its eyes, joined the cocks in heralding the new-born day. Presently the peafowl, who were roosting on the giant *samal* trees, scattered over

the wide grass area, added their piercing call to the growing
volume of jungle sounds, and when the rising sun touched the
topmost branches of a *samal* tree within our view, the twenty
or more peafowl that were clustered on the widespreading
branches flew down among the plum bushes. Getting to his
feet Tom knocked the ashes out of his pipe, and said it was
time for us to enter the jungle. The dew in this low-lying area
rises to a height of about thirty feet, and when going through
tree jungle in the early morning the moisture dripping from
the leaves resembles both in sound and in volume a shower of
rain. The grass, waist-high for Tom and chin-high for me, into
which we stepped from the road was saturated with dew and we
had only gone a few yards into it when my clothes were clinging
to me, and adding to the discomfort of wet clothes the morning
was bitterly cold.

Going in the direction of the *samal* tree we put up ten or a
dozen peafowl all of which, with one exception, flew low for
some distance and resettled in the grass. The exception, a peacock
in full plumage, rose at a steep angle and alighted on a branch
of the *samal* tree. Tom now filled me with delight by putting his
12-bore breach-loading hammer gun into my hands, and telling
me to go forward and shoot the peacock. I had a distance of a
hundred and fifty yards to go and when I had covered forty
yards I stopped, and as I was trying to cock the gun I heard a
low whistle and on looking round saw Tom beckoning to me.
On my rejoining him he said I was out of range where I had
stopped, and when I told him I had not stopped to fire the gun,
but to cock it, he said I must never cock a gun until I was ready
to fire for it was dangerous anywhere to carry a cocked gun
and most of all in grass where one was liable to trip up or stumble
into unseen holes. 'Now,' he said, 'go forward and have another
try.' On this second occasion—taking advantage of a big plum

bush—I crept up to within easy range. The *samal* tree was leafless but was covered with big red flowers, and sitting on a branch on my side of the tree, with the slanting rays of the sun shining on it, was the most beautiful peacock I had ever seen. The time had now come to cock the gun but what with excitement and my frozen fingers I found it impossible to draw back the hammers, and while I was wondering what to do next the peacock flew away. 'Never mind,' Tom said when he came up to me. 'You will have better luck next time.' But no more birds obliged me by flying into trees that morning, and after Tom had shot a red jungle-cock and three peafowl we left the grass and plum jungle and regaining the road made for home and a late breakfast.

chapter three

WITH THE THREE LESSONS I have detailed,
my jungle training—as far as my elders were
concerned—was over. I had been shown how to
handle and to fire a gun, and I had been taken
into jungles in which there were tigers and bears
with the object, I believe, of showing me that no
danger was to be apprehended from unwounded
animals. Lessons well learnt when young are
never afterwards forgotten, and I had learnt my
lessons well. Whether or not from now onwards
I took advantage of these lessons to interest myself
in any form of field sport was entirely my own
concern, and I am glad it was so. I am glad the
decision was left with me and that I was not
told I must do this or must do that not because
of any desire on my part, but because my elders
considered it was the right thing for a boy of
my age to do.

Boys are not lacking in intelligence, and where

facilities for field sports exist—as they do in most parts of India—they should not be deprived of the pleasure of selecting the form of sport that most appeals to them and for which they are physically fitted, or of eschewing field sports altogether if they have no interest in them and are averse to taking life. Compulsion—no matter how well veiled—even though it follows the lines of an individual's inclinations, takes, in my opinion, all the joy out of any form of sport.

Tom helped my mother and my sisters to nurse me through a life-and-death struggle with pneumonia, and when an incentive was needed to make me take an interest in the life that had so nearly slipped through my fingers, he gave me my first catapult. Sitting on my bed Tom produced the catapult from his pocket, and putting it into my hands, took a cup of beef juice off the bed-side table and told me I must drink it in order to get strong enough to use the catapult. Thereafter I took without protest all that was offered me, and as I regained strength Tom assisted the other members of the family to keep my interest alive by telling me about the jungles and instructing me in the use of my catapult.

From Tom I learned that the year—for sportsmen—was divided into two seasons, a close season and an open season. During the close season my catapult would have to be put away, for at this time birds were nesting and it was cruel to kill them while they were sitting on their eggs or caring for their young. During the open season I could use my catapult freely to kill birds, provided I made use of every bird I killed. Green pigeons and blue rockpigeons, which abounded in our hills, could be shot to eat, but all other birds would have to be skinned and set up and for this purpose, when the time came, Tom provided me with a skinning knife and a pot of arsenical soap. Tom did not include taxidermy among his many accomplishments, however, but his demonstration with a cock *kalege* pheasant as subject gave me a general idea of how to remove a bird's skin, and practice later made me perfect. A cousin of ours, Stephen Dease, was at that time compiling a book of the birds of Kumaon and most of the four hundred and eighty coloured illustrations in his book were made from birds in my collection, or from specimens I specially collected for him.

Tom had two dogs: Poppy, a red pi dog which he found starving in the streets of Kabul during the second Afghan war and which he brought back to India with him; and Magog, a liver and white spaniel with a great plume of a tail. Poppy had no use for small boys, but Magog—who was strong enough to carry me for short distances—was more liberal minded and in addition to constituting himself my protector, lavished all his affection on me. It was Magog who taught me it was unwise to pass close to dense cover in which animals who were sleeping might resent being disturbed, and it was he who showed me that a dog can learn to walk as noiselessly through a jungle as a cat. With Magog to give me confidence I penetrated deep into the jungles where previously I had been afraid to go, and during the catapult days we met with one exciting experience which nearly cost Magog his life.

We were out that morning trying to get a scarlet sun-bird for my collection when Dansay, out for a walk with his Scottie called Thistle, joined us. The two dogs were not good friends, but they refrained from fighting and after we had proceeded a short distance together Thistle put up a porcupine and Magog,

disregarding my urgent call to him, joined in the chase. Dansay
was armed with his muzzle-loading shotgun but was afraid to
use it for fear of hitting the dogs which were running one on
either side of the porcupine and biting at it. Running was not
Dansay's strong point and, further, he was hampered with his
gun so it was not long before the porcupine, the two dogs, and
I, had left him far behind. Porcupines are very unpleasant
animals to deal with, for though they cannot project or 'shoot'
their quills they are tough and very agile on their feet, and
their method of defence, or attack, is to erect their quills and
run backwards.

Before joining in the chase I had stuffed my catapult into
my pocket and armed myself with a stout stick, but I was able
to do little to help the dogs, for every time I got near the
porcupine it ran at me and I was several times saved by the dogs
from being impaled on its quills. When the chase had covered
half a mile and we were approaching a deep ravine in which
there were porcupine burrows, Magog got the porcupine by
the nose and Thistle got hold of its throat. Dansay arrived when
the fight was practically over, and, for good measure, he put a
charge of shot into the porcupine. Both dogs were streaming
with blood, and after we had pulled from them all the quills we
could we hurried home—Dansay carrying the porcupine slung
over his shoulder—to try to pull out with pincers the quills
that had broken off short and resisted all our attempts to pull
them out with our fingers, for porcupine quills are barbed and
difficult to extract.

Magog passed a very restless day and night sneezing frequently
and, each time he did so, leaving a big clot of blood on the
straw on which he was lying. The following day was fortunately
a Sunday and when Tom arrived from Naini Tal to spend the
day at home, he found that a quill had broken off short inside

Magog's nose. After many fruitless attempts Tom eventually got hold of the broken end with the princers and extracted a six-inch length of quill, of the thickness of the quills that are used for the making of penholders. Blood spurted out after the quill had been removed, and as we had no means of stopping the flow Magog's life was despaired of. However, with careful nursing and feeding he recovered, as did also Thistle who had not come as badly out of the fight with the porcupine as Magog had done.

After I had been given the muzzle-loading gun, about which I shall tell you later, Magog and I met with two exciting experiences, one at Kaladhungi and the other at Naini Tal. Naya Gaon village, which I have mentioned elsewhere, was at that time fully cultivated and between the cultivation and the Dhunigar stream there was a strip of jungle, intercepted with open glades. Through this strip of jungle which was from a quarter to half a mile wide runs a game track parallel to, and midway between, the cultivation and the stream. The jungles on both sides of the stream were teeming with game in the way of red jungle-fowl, peafowl, deer, and pig, that took heavy toll of the crops and that crossed the game track on their way to or from the fields. It was on this game track that Magog and I met with our first experience.

Naya Gaon is three miles from our home at Kaladhungi and at crack of dawn one morning Magog and I set out to try to bag a peafowl. Keeping to the middle of the wide road, for the light was not good and the jungle through which the road ran was the haunt of leopards and tigers, we arrived at the point where the game track met the road just as the sun was rising. Here I proceeded to load the gun, a long business, for first the powder had to be measured and poured down the barrel and a thick felt wad firmly rammed down on it. The shot then had to be measured and poured down on to the felt wad and a thin cardboard wad rammed down on the shot. When the ramrod bounced off the charge in the barrel, the gun was considered to be well and truly loaded. The big cumbersome hammer was then put at half-cock and a percussion cap firmly fixed on the nipple. When these several items had been performed to my satisfaction I stowed away the loading materials in my haversack, and Magog and I set off on the game track. A number of jungle-fowl and several peafowl crossed the track in front of us but none of them stood to give me a shot, and we had proceeded for about half a mile when we came to an open glade and as we stepped out on it seven peafowl, in single file, crossed its further end. Waiting for a few moments we crept forward to where the peafowl had crossed, and I then sent in Magog to put them up.

Peafowl when put up by a dog in thick jungle invariably settle on the branches of trees, and as I was at the stage when even a sitting bird was difficult to shoot, it took Magog's and my combined efforts to bring a peafowl to bag. Magog loved peafowl above all other game, and after treeing the birds he invariably dashed round barking at them, and while he engaged their attention I crept up to do my part.

The seven peafowl after crossing the glade had evidently taken to their legs, for Magog had gone at least a hundred yards into the dense scrub and tree jungle before I heard a flutter of wings and the squark of the peafowl, followed immediately afterwards by a frightened yelp from Magog and the angry roar of a tiger. The peafowl had quite evidently led Magog on to a sleeping tiger, and birds, dog, and tiger, were each expressing their surprise, fear, and resentment, in their own particular way. Magog after his first yelp of fear was barking furiously and running, and the tiger was emitting roar upon roar and chasing him, and both were coming towards me. In the general confusion a peacock—giving its alarm call—came sailing through the trees and alighted on a branch just above my head, but for the time being I had lost all interest in birds and my one and only desire was to go somewhere, far away, where there were no tigers. Magog had four legs to carry him over the ground whereas I only had two, so without any feeling of shame—for deserting a faithful companion—I picked up my feet and ran as I had never run before. Magog soon overtook me and the roaring behind us ceased.

I can picture the tiger now, though I could not do so at the time, sitting down on his haunches on reaching the open glade and laughing, a tiger's laugh, at the sight of a big dog and a small boy running for what they thought was dear life, while all that he was doing was to shoo away a dog that had disturbed his slumbers.

I met with one more experience that winter before we left Kaladhungi for our summer home in Naini Tal and on that occasion I was alone, for Magog had taken french leave to visit a lady friend in the village and was absent when I started. I had been avoiding dense jungle for some time and keeping to more open stretches, and on this particular morning I was looking for jungle-fowl near the Garuppu road below Naya Gaon. Many birds were scratching about on the road but none of them let me get close enough for a shot, so I left the road and entered the jungle which here consisted of trees, a few scattered bushes, and short grass. Before leaving the road I removed my shoes and stockings, and I had only proceeded a short distance when I caught sight of a red jungle-cock scratching up the dead leaves under a tree.

When a jungle-fowl, or a farmyard chicken, scratches up in the one case dead leaves and in the other litter, it holds its head

high when looking round for danger and if there is no danger
near it lowers its head to feed on the exposed insects or corn.
The cock that was feeding under the tree was out of range so I
started on my bare feet to stalk it. Gaining a yard or two each
time the cock lowered his head and freezing each time he raised
it, I had nearly got within shooting range when I came on a
shallow depression. One step into the depression—which was
masked on both sides with knee-high grass—and two steps on
the far side and I would be in range, and would in addition
have a small tree against which to rest the heavy gun and take
careful aim. So waiting until the cock again lowered his head I
stepped into the depression, *and put my bare foot on the coils of a
big python*. A few days previously I had run as no boy had ever
run, and I now jumped as no boy had ever jumped, and as I
landed on the far side of the depression I whipped round and
fired into the writhing mass and ran until I regained the safety
of the road.

In all the years I have spent in the jungles of Northern India
I have never heard of a python killing a human being; even so,
I know I had a very lucky escape that
morning, for if the python
had caught me by the leg,
as it would undoubtedly
have done if it had not
been asleep, there would have
been no necessity for it to kill me, for
I should have died of fright, as a full-grown
cheetal hind died near my tent one night
when a python caught it by the tail. How big the python was
that I stepped on, and whether I killed it or not, I do not
know for I never went back to look. In that same area I have
seen python eighteen feet in length, and I have seen one that

had swallowed a *cheetal* and another that had swallowed a *kakar*.

Magog and I met with our second experience shortly after we returned to Naini Tal from Kaladhungi. The forests round Naini Tal at that time teemed with *kalege* pheasants and game of all kinds, and as there were few sportsmen and no restrictions with regard to shooting areas it was possible for Magog and me to go out in the evening after school hours and bag a brace of pheasants or hill-partridge for the larder.

One evening Magog and I walked down the Kaladhungi road and though Magog put up several pheasants, none of them remained seated on a tree long enough to give me a shot. At Sarya Tal, the little lake nestling at the foot of the valley, we left the road and entered the jungle with the object of working back to the gorge at the upper end of the valley. Near the lake I shot a pheasant, and going through dense brushwood and over great piles of rocks we had got back to within two hundred yards of the road when, on emerging from some thick cover on to an open grassy glade, we saw several pheasants jumping up from a bed of wild balsam to eat the berries off a low bush. The birds were only visible while they were in the air, and as I had not reached the stage when I could hit a moving target I sat down on the ground, with Magog lying alongside, to wait for one of the birds to come out on to the glade.

We had been in position for some time and the birds were still jumping up to reach the berries when on the road—which ran diagonally across the face of the hill—we heard a number of men talking and laughing. From the rattling of their tin cans I knew they were milkmen who had been up to Naini Tal to sell milk and were now on their way home to their villages below Sarya Tal. I first heard the men when they turned a corner in the road four hundred yards away, and they had reached a point above and a little to our left front when they all shouted together as though they were driving some animal off the road. Next minute, in the jungle immediately above us, we heard some big animal coming in our direction. The undergrowth was too dense for me to see what the animal was until it dashed into the bed of balsam and put up the pheasants, which went skimming over our heads: then out on to the open glade bounded a big leopard. The leopard saw us while he was still in the air, and as he touched the ground he lay flat and froze in that position. The glade sloped upwards at an angle of thirty degrees, and as the leopard was above and some ten yards from us every inch of him from his chin to the tip of his tail was visible. As the leopard appeared I released my left hand from the gun and placed it on Magog's neck and I could now feel tremors running through him, as I could feel them running through myself.

This was the first leopard that Magog and I had ever seen, and as the wind was blowing up the hill I believe our reactions to it were much the same—intense excitement, but no feeling of fear. This absence of fear I can now, after a lifetime's experience, attribute to the fact that the leopard had no evil intentions towards us. Driven off the road by the men, he was quite possibly making for the mass of rocks over which Magog and I had recently come, and on clearing the bushes and finding a boy and a dog directly in his line of retreat he had frozen, to take stock of the situation. A glance at us was sufficient to satisfy him that we had no hostile intensions towards him, for a leopard can size up a situation more quickly than any other animal in our jungles. And now, satisfied from our whole attitude that he had nothing to fear from us, and satisfied also that

there were no other human beings in the direction that he wanted
to go, he leapt from his crouching position and in a few graceful
bounds disappeared into the jungle behind us. The wind blowing
from this direction carried the scent of the leopard to Magog
and in a second he was on his feet growling fiercely and with
all the hair on his neck and back on end. Only now he realized
that the beautiful animal he had watched without any feeling
of fear and that could have killed him, big as he was, without
any difficulty, had been a leopard, his most deadly and most
feared enemy in all the jungles.

chapter four

BETWEEN THE CATAPULT AND THE muzzle-loader periods there was a bow-and-arrow interlude which I look back on with very great pleasure, for though I never succeeded in impaling bird or beast with an arrow I opened my credit account—with my small savings—with the bank of Nature during that period, and the Jungle Lore I absorbed during the interlude, and later, has been a never-ending source of pleasure to me.

I have used the word 'absorbed', in preference to 'learnt', for jungle lore is not a science that can be learnt from textbooks; it can, however, be absorbed, a little at a time, and the absorption process can go on indefinitely, for the book of nature has no beginning, as it has no end. Open the book where you will, and at any period of your life, and if you have the desire to acquire knowledge you will find it of intense interest, and no matter how long or how intently you study the pages your interest will not flag, for in nature there is no finality.

Today it is spring, and the tree before you is bedecked with gay bloom. Attracted by this bloom a multitude of birds of many colours are flitting from branch to branch, some drinking the nectar from the flowers, others eating the petals, and others again feeding on the bees that are busily collecting honey. Tomorrow the bloom will have given place to fruit and a different multitude of birds will be in possession of the tree. And each member of the different multitudes has its allotted place in the scheme of nature. One to beautify nature's garden, another to fill it with melody, and yet another to regenerate the garden.

Season after season, year after year, the scene changes. A new generation of birds in varying numbers and species adorn the tree. The tree loses a limb—torn off in a storm—gets stackheaded and dies, and another tree takes its place; and so the cycle goes on.

On the path at your feet is the track of a snake that passed that way an hour before sunrise. The snake was going from the right-hand side of the path to the left, was three inches in girth, and you can be reasonably certain that it was of a poisonous variety. Tomorrow the track on the same path, or on another, may show that the snake that crossed it five minutes earlier was travelling from left to right, that it was five inches in girth, and that it was non-poisonous.

And so the knowledge you absorb today will be added to the knowledge you will absorb tomorrow, and on your capacity for absorption, not on any fixed standard, will depend the amount of knowledge you ultimately accumulate. And at the end of the accumulating period—be that period one year or fifty—you will find that you are only at the beginning, and that the whole field of nature lies before you waiting to be explored and to be absorbed. But be assured that if you are not interested, or if you have no desire to acquire knowledge, you will learn nothing from nature.

I walked with a companion for twelve miles through a beautiful forest from one camp to another. It was the month of April and nature was at her best. Trees, shrubs, and creepers were in full bloom. Gaily coloured butterflies flitted from flower to flower, and the air, filled with the scent of the flowers, throbbed with the song of birds. At the end of the day my companion was asked if he had enjoyed the walk, and he answered, 'No. The road was very rough.'

I was travelling, shortly after World War I, from Bombay to Mombasa in the British India liner *Karagola*. There were five of us on the upper deck. I was going to Tanganyika to build a house, the other four were going to Kenya—three to shoot and one to look at a farm he had purchased. The sea was rough and I am a bad sailor, so I spent most of my time dozing in a corner of the smoke room. The others sat at a table nearby playing bridge, smoking, and talking, mostly about sport. One day, on being awakened by a cramp in my leg, I heard the youngest member of the party say, 'Oh, I know all about tigers. I spent a fortnight with a Forest Officer in the Central Provinces last year.'

Admittedly two extreme cases, but they will serve to emphasize my contention that if you are not interested you will see nothing but the road you walk on, and if you have no desire to acquire knowledge and assume you can learn in a fortnight what cannot be learnt in a lifetime, you will remain ignorant to the end.

chapter five

DURING MY CHILDHOOD DAYS, AND the ten years I spent at school, and again while I was working in Bengal, and later between the two world wars, I spent all my holidays and leave in the jungles in and around Kaladhungi. If during those years I did not absorb as much jungle lore as I might have done, the fault is mine, for I had ample opportunities of doing so. Opportunities which will never be enjoyed by another, for pressure of population has brought under cultivation large areas on which in my time game wandered at will; while standardization of forests, with all the evils it brings in its train of wild life, has resulted in the total destruction of the trees that bore the flowers and the fruit that birds and animals live on. One result of this destruction, which in my opinion was quite unnecessary, has been to drive millions of monkeys out of the forests on to cultivated land,

presenting Government with a problem which they are finding it difficult to deal with owing to the religious prejudices of the population, who look upon monkeys as sacred animals. A day will come when this problem will have to be faced, and the lot of those who have to face it will not be an enviable one, for in the United Provinces alone the monkey population—in my opinion—is less than ten million, and ten million monkeys living on crops and garden fruit present a very major problem.

Had I realized in those far-off days that a time would come when I would write this book, I would have tried to learn more than I did, for the time I spent in the jungles held unalloyed happiness for me, and that happiness I would now gladly share. My happiness, I believe, resulted from the fact that all wild life is happy in its natural surroundings. In nature there is no sorrow, and no repining. A bird from a flock, or an animal from a herd, is taken by hawk or by carnivorous beast and those that are left rejoice that their time had not come today, and have no thought of tomorrow. When I was ignorant I tried to rescue birds and young animals caught by hawks or by eagles, and deer caught by carnivorous beasts, but soon found that in trying to rescue one I caused the death of two. For the talons of hawk and eagle, and the teeth and claws of carnivorous beasts, hold poison in the form of decayed flesh or blood, and unless expert treatment is immediately applied—which is not possible in a jungle—only one in a hundred of rescued birds or animals survive, and the killer, being deprived of its prey, immediately finds another victim to satisfy its hunger or the hunger of its young.

It is the function of certain birds and animals to maintain the balance in nature, and in order to carry out this function and at the same time provide themselves with the only food they can assimilate it is necessary for them to kill. This killing is— whenever possible—expeditiously and very expertly performed. From the killer's point of view expeditious killing is necessary to avoid attracting enemies, and I see no reason why it should not also be a provision of nature designed to minimize suffering.

Each species has its own method of killing and the method employed in individual cases depends to a great extent on the relative size of the killer and its victim. For instance, a peregrine falcon that does most of its killing on the ground will, on occasion, take a small bird on the wing and kill and eat it in the air. Again, a tiger that on occasion finds it necessary to hamstring an animal before overpowering and killing it will on another occasion strike down a victim with a single blow.

The jungle folk, *in their natural surroundings,* do not kill wantonly. Killing for sport is, however, occasionally indulged in, and some animals, notably pine-marten, civet cats, and mongoose, will, *in abnormal circumstances,* kill in excess of their needs. Sport has a wide meaning and can be interpreted in many ways. In the two instances I am going to narrate it should be interpreted liberally.

When Percy Wyndham was Commissioner of Kumaon he was asked by Sir Harcourt Butler, Governor of the then United Provinces, to provide a python for the recently-opened Lucknow Zoo. Wyndham was on his winter tour when he received the request and on arrival at Kaladhungi he asked me if I knew of a python that would be a credit to our jungles and a suitable gift for a commissioner to present to a Governor. It so happened that I did know of such a python, and next day Wyndham and two of his *shikaris* and I set out on an elephant to look at the python I had in mind. I had known this python for several years and I had no difficulty in guiding the elephant to it.

We found the python lying full stretch on the bed of a shallow stream with an inch or two of gin-clear water flowing over it, and it looked for all the world like a museum specimen in a glass case. When Wyndham saw it he said it was just the kind of python he had hoped to secure, and he ordered the mahout to undo a length of rope from the trappings of the elephant. When this had been done, Wyndham made a noose at one end of the rope and handing it to the *shikaris* told them to dismount from the elephant and noose the snake. With an exclamation of horror the two men said it would be *quite* impossible for them to do this. 'Don't be frightened,' Wyndham said, adding that if the snake showed any sign of attacking them he would shoot it—he was armed with a heavy rifle. This, however, did not appeal to the men, so turning to me Wyndham asked me if I would like to help them. Very emphatically I assured him there was nothing in all the world that I would like less, so handing his rifle to me he joined the two men on the ground.

I greatly regret that instead of the rifle I did not have a movie camera in my hands to make a record of the following few minutes, for I have never witnessed a more amusing scene. Wyndham's plan was to noose the python's tail and haul it to

dry land, and then tie it up so that it could be loaded on to
the elephant. When he explained this plan to the two *shikaris*
they handed the noose to Wyndhom and said that if he would
pass the noose under the snake's tail they would haul on the
rope. Wyndham, however, was firm in his opinion that the
noosing could be done more expertly by the *shikaris*. Eventually,
after a lot of advancing and retreating and dumb play to avoid
alarming the python, all three men entered the water, each
attempting to hold the rope as far away from the noose as
possible, and very gingerly they approached the python upstream.
When they got to within an arm's length of it, and while each
was urging the other to take the noose and pass it under the tail,
the python raised its head a foot or two out of the water, and
started to turn and glide towards them. With a yell of '*Bhago
Sahib*' ('Run sir') the *shikaris* splashed out of the water, followed
by Wyndham, and all three dashed into the thick brushwood
on the side of the stream while the python glided under the
roots of a big *jamun* tree and disappeared from view, and the
mahout and I nearly fell off the elephant laughing.

A month later I received a letter from Wyndham informing
me he was arriving in Kaladhungi the following day, and that
he would like to have another try to capture the python. Geoff
Hopkins and a friend of his who had recently arrived from
England were with me when I received the letter, and the
three of us set off to see if the python was still in the place
where I had last seen it. Near the tree under the roots of
which the python lived was a *sambhar*'s stamping ground. On
this ground, the earth of which had been churned to fine
dust by the hooves of generations of *sambhar*, we found the
python lying dead, killed a few minutes before our arrival by
a pair of otters.

The method employed by otters in killing python, and also crocodiles, for sport—for I have never known of their using either of these reptiles for food—is to approach, one on either side of their intended victim. When the python or crocodile turns its head to defend itself against the attack of, say, the otter on the right, the otter on the left jumps in—otter are very agile— and takes a bite at the victim's neck as close to its head as possible. Then when the victim turns and tries to defend itself against its assailant on the left the one on the right jumps in and takes a bite. In this way, biting alternately and a little at a time, the neck of the victim is bitten away right down to the bone before it is dispatched, for both python and crocodiles are very tenacious of life.

In the case I am narrating the python measured 17 feet 6 inches in length and 26 inches in girth, and the pair of otters must have run a considerable risk while killing it. Otter, however, are big-hearted animals and quite possibly—like human beings—they value their sport in proportion to the risk involved.

The second instance concerns a big bull elephant and a pair of tigers, and unless my theory of 'sport' is accepted I can give no reason for the encounter between the lord and the king and queen of the Indian jungle. The encounter received wide publicity in the Indian press and many letters on the subject were written by renowned sportsmen to the editors of *The Pioneer* and *The Statesman*. The theories advanced for the encounter were: old vendetta, revenge for the killing of a cub, and killing for food. None of the writers of the articles and letters witnessed the encounter, and as a similar case from which deductions might have been made had never been known, the theories remained just theories and proved nothing.

I first heard of the encounter between the elephant and the tigers, which resulted in the death of the elephant, when the Superintendent, Tarai, and Bhabar asked me if it would take 200 gallons of paraffin oil to cremate the body of an elephant. Inquiries at the Superintendent's office in Naini Tal elicited the information that an elephant had been killed by the tigers at Tanakpur on rocky ground where it could not be buried, hence the claim for the cost of cremating it. This information was intensely interesting to me hut unfortunately the trail was ten days old, and, further, the evidence had been burnt and heavy rain had obliterated all tracks.

The Naib-Tahsildar of Tanakpur, who had heard but not witnessed the encounter, was a friend of mine and I am indebted to him for the particulars that enable me to narrate the incident.

Tanakpur, terminus of a branch line of the Oudh-Tirhut Railway and a trading centre of considerable importance, is situated on the right bank of the Sarda river where it emerges from the foothills. Thirty years ago the river flowed along the foot of the high bank on which Tanakpur is built, but like all big rivers where they leave the foothills the Sarda keeps making new channels for itself, and at the time these events took place the river was two miles from Tanakpur. Between the main bank, which is about a hundred feet high, and the river there were several small channels and on the islands formed by these channels there was moderate to heavy tree, scrub, and grass jungle.

One day two *malhas* (boatmen) living in Tanakpur went to the Sarda river to net fish. They stayed out longer than they had intended and the sun was setting when they started on their two-mile walk home. On emerging from a dense patch of grass on to the last channel that lay between them and the high bank, they saw two tigers standing on the far side of the channel, which here was about forty yards wide, with a trickle of water

in it, and as the tigers were between them and their objective the men crouched down where they were, intending to wait until the tigers moved away. These men had seen tigers on many occasions and were not unduly alarmed. This point is important for when anyone suffers from nerves in a jungle, imagination is liable to play strange tricks. At this stage of the proceedings there was still a little light from the recently set sun, and the full moon having just risen behind the two men the tigers standing on the open ground were in clear view. Presently there was a movement in the grass through which they had just come and out on to their side of the channel, stepped an elephant with big tusks. This tusker was well known in the Tanakpur forests and it had made itself unpopular with the Forest Department owing to its habit of pulling down the pillars supporting the roof of the Chene forest bungalow. It was not, however, a rogue in the sense of molesting human beings.

When the elephant stepped out on to the channel and saw the tigers on the far side it raised its trunk and trumpeted and

started to move towards them. The tigers now turned to face
the elephant and as it approached them one demonstrated in
front of it while the other circled round behind and sprang on
its back. Swinging its head round, the elephant tried to get at
the tiger on its back with its trunk, and the one in front then
sprang on to its head. The elephant was now screaming with
rage, while the tigers were giving vent to full-throated roars. When
tigers roar with anger it is a very terrifying sound, and since
the screaming of the maddened elephant was added to this
terrifying sound, it is little wonder that the *malhas* lost their
nerve and, abandoning their nets and catch of fish, sprinted
for Tanakpur at their best speed.

In Tanakpur preparations were being made for the evening
meal when the sounds of the fight were first heard. Shortly
thereafter, when the *malhas* arrived with the news that an
elephant and two tigers were fighting, a few bold spirits went
to the edge of the high bank to try to see the fight. When it
was realized, however, that the contestants were coming towards
them, a stampede took place and in a few minutes every door in
Tanakpur was fast closed. Opinions on the duration of the fight
differed. Some maintained that it lasted all night, while others
maintained that it ended at midnight. Mr Matheson, a retired
gentleman whose bungalow was on the high bank immediately
above where the fight took place, said it lasted for many hours,
and that he had never heard more appalling or terrifying sounds.
Guns shots were heard during the night, but it is not clear
whether they were fired by the police or by Mr Matheson; anyway,
they did not have the desired effect of stopping the fight and
driving the animals away.

In the morning the residents of Tanakpur again assembled
on the high ground, and at the foot of the hundred-foot
boulder-strewn bank they saw the elephant lying dead. From
the injuries described by the Naib-Tahsildar, it was evident that

it had died of loss of blood. No portion of the elephant had
been eaten, and no dead or injured tigers were found at the
time or subsequently in the vicinity of Tanakpur.

I do not think that the tigers, at the onset, had any intention
of killing the elephant. The theory of an old vendetta, anger at
the killing of a cub, and killing for food are not convincing. The
fact remains, however, that a big bull elephant, carrying tusks
weighing ninety pounds, was killed near Tanakpur by two tigers
and I am of the opinion that what started as a lark—by a pair
of mating tigers when an elephant tried to shoo them out of his
way—developed into a real fight. I am also of the opinion that
when the second tiger sprang on the elephant's head it clawed
out the elephant's eyes and that thereafter the blinded animal
dashed about aimlessly until it came to the high bank. Here on
the round loose boulders, which afforded no foothold, it was
practically anchored and at the mercy of the tigers who—possibly
because of injuries received in the fight—showed no mercy.

All carnivorous animals kill their victims with their teeth,
and those that stalk their prey depend on their claws not only
to catch and hold but also, on occasion, to disable a victim before
dispatching it with their teeth. The act of killing, except in the
case of animals that run down their prey, is so seldom witnessed
in the jungles, and, when witnessed, the initial movements of
the killer are so rapid and consequently so difficult to follow
that after witnessing, possibly, twenty kills by tigers and leopards
I can give no precise description of the movements of the killer
at the actual moment of contact with its victim. In only one of
the cases I have witnessed—a *cheetal* hind feeding down-wind—
was a head-on attack made. This is understandable, for the horns
of the animals usually killed by tigers and leopards are capable
of inflicting very serious wounds. The attacks in the other cases
witnessed were made by the killers coming up from behind, or
at an angle, and with a single spring or short rush getting hold

of their victims with their claws, and then with a lightning-fast movement seizing them by the throat and bringing them to the ground.

In bringing an animal to the ground great care has to be exercised, for a full-grown *sambhar* or *cheetal* could with a single kick disembowel a tiger or a leopard. To avoid injury, and also to prevent the victim from struggling to its feet, the head, in the act of pulling it to the ground, is twisted round, as shown in the sketch. When an animal is thus brought down and held it can kick indefinitely without doing its assailant any injury, and it cannot rise or roll over without dislocating its neck. It occasionally happens that when a heavy animal is brought to the ground the fall dislocates the neck, and it also occasionally happens that the neck is dislocated by the canine teeth of the assailant. When the neck is not dislocated either by its fall or by the attacker's teeth, the victim is killed by strangulation.

I have never seen an animal hamstrung by a leopard, but have seen many cases of hamstringing by tigers. In all those cases

the hamstringing was done by the claws and not by the teeth of
tigers. A friend once brought me news of the killing of one of
his cows on the Semdhar ridge six miles from Naini Tal. He owned
a big herd of cattle and had seen many kills by tigers and leopards
and from the absence of injuries on this particular cow's neck
and from the way the flesh had been torn in shreds he suspected
that it had been killed and partly eaten by some unknown animal.
The day was still young when he brought me the news, and
two hours later we arrived at the kill. The cow, a full-grown
animal, had been killed on a fifty-foot-wide fire track and no
attempt had been made to drag it away. When the condition of
the kill had been described to me I had come to the conclusion
that the cow had been killed by a Himalayan black bear.
Bears are not habitual meat-eaters
but they do occasionally kill,
and not being equipped
for killing, as tigers and
leopards are, their
method of killing is very
clumsy. The cow had
not been killed by a
bear, however, but by a
tiger, and killed in a very unusual way. It had first been
hamstrung, and then killed by being disembowelled. Having
killed the cow the tiger had eaten a portion of the hindquarters
by tearing away the flesh with its claws. Tracking on the hard
ground was not possible, so I spent the rest of the day searching
the surrounding forests to try to get a shot at the tiger on foot.
Near sundown I returned to the kill and sat up over it all night
on the branch of a tree. The tiger did not return to his kill, nor
did he return to the kills of nine other animals—six cows and
three young buffaloes—that he killed in identically the same way.

This method of killing was intensely cruel from a human being's point of view, but not from the point of view of the tiger. He had to kill to provide himself with food, and his method of killing was dependent on his physical condition. The fact that the tiger could not use his canine teeth to kill, or to drag away his kills, and that he had to use his claws instead of his teeth to tear the flesh from his kills, was proof that he was suffering from some physical defect. This defect, I am convinced, had resulted from a carelessly fired high velocity bullet having shot away a portion of his lower jaw. I came to this conviction on seeing the tiger's first kill and my conviction—that he was wounded and that he was still suffering from his wound—was strengthened by the lengthening period between the kills, and the fact that he was able to eat less from each succeeding kill. His wound had evidently been received over a kill and this would account for his never returning for a second meal. The killing stopped after the tenth kill and as no tiger was shot or found dead in that area I am inclined to think that the tiger crawled away into a cave, of which there were many on a nearby hill, and there succumbed to his wound.

Admittedly this was an unusual case, but it was not the only case I know of hamstringing, for two of the biggest buffaloes I have ever seen killed by tigers had been hamstrung by the claws of tigers before being pulled down and killed by the tiger's teeth.

chapter six

WHEN THE RUBBER OF THE catapult Tom
gave me perished, I made myself a pellet bow.
The difference between a bow that shoots a
pellet and one that shoots an arrow is that the
former is shorter and stiffer, and that it has two
strings between which a small square of webbing
is fixed to hold the pellet. Practice is needed to
shoot with a pellet bow, for if the wrist of the
hand holding the bow is not turned at the exact
moment that the pellet is released, very serious
injury can result to the thumb of the bow hand.
A pellet bow can shoot with twice the velocity
that a catapult can, but it is not as accurate as
a catapult. The Naini Tal Treasury, which was
guarded by Gurkhas of the Regular Army, was
just across the road from our summer home.
The Gurkhas were keen pellet bowmen and I
was often invited into the Treasury grounds to
compete with them. In the grounds was a short

wooden post on which was hung a great circular gong for
striking the hours. On this post a match-box used to be placed
and from a range of twenty yards the man selected to compete
with me, and I, each fired one shot in turn. The *Havildar* of
the guard, a short stocky man as strong as a bull, was the best
shot of them all, but—much to the delight of the onlookers—
he never succeeded in beating me.

Necessity compelled me to use a pellet bow, and though I
acquired sufficient accuracy with it to continue my collection
of birds, I never took to it as I had taken to a catapult, and
after reading Fennimore Cooper's thrilling books I supplemented
my pellet bow with a bow to project arrows. If Cooper's Red
Indians could shoot game with an arrow, I saw no reason why
I should not be able to do the same. The people in our part of
India do not use bows and arrows so I had no pattern to work
on; however, after several attempts I made a bow to my liking
and with this bow and two arrows—tipped with sharp nails—
I set out to emulate a Red Indian. I had no illusions about the
killing powers of my arrows, or their defensive value, so I walked
warily, for in addition to the jungle fowl and peafowl that I hoped
to shoot, there were in our jungles many animals of which I
was mightily afraid. To enable me to approach the game I wanted
to shoot, and to assist me in seeking protection in trees when
danger threatened, I discarded my shoes, for there were no
thin rubber-soled shoes in those days and the choice lay between
bare feet and hard leather shoes which were neither suitable for
stalking in nor for climbing trees.

Two watercourses, dry except after heavy rain, ran down
from the foothills and met at the lower end of our estate. Both
had sandy beds and in the jungle between them, which was a
quarter of a mile wide at the bottom end, a mile wide at the top
end, and two miles long, was game of all kinds. The canal in

which the girls bathed formed a boundary between our estate
and the jungle, and I had only to cross it by a fallen tree to get
in touch with the game, which included the birds I hoped to
shoot. In later years, when I had a cine-camera, I spent many
days on a tree on our side of the canal, trying to film tigers that
came down to the canal to drink. And it was in this jungle that
I shot my last tiger, on my release from the army after Hitler's
war. The tiger killed—at different times—a horse, a calf, and
two bullocks, and as it resisted all my attempts to drive it away
I shot it. Sister Maggie doubted my ability to hold a rifle steady,
for many forms of malaria contracted in many jungles had, she
thought, impaired the steadiness of my hands. However, to make
quite sure of my shot I called the tiger up for judgement, found
it guilty, and shot it through the eye as it was looking at me at
the range of a few feet. It was murder, of course, but justifiable
murder; for though I was willing to let the tiger live in the dense
patch of lantana it had selected for its home—two hundred
yards from the village—and pay compensation for all the animals
it killed, it was difficult to replace these animals owing to the
country-wide shortage of farm animals bought about by the
war, and—as I have said—the tiger resisted all my attempts to
drive it away.

Magog and I had explored the strip of jungle between the
two watercourses very thoroughly and I knew all the places to
be avoided; even so, I did not consider it was safe to cross the
canal by the fallen tree and go hunting jungle-fowl and peafowl
until I had satisfied myself that there were no tigers in it. And
this I did by examining the watercourse on the left-hand side
of the jungle. The tigers that frequented the strip invariably came
from the west at about sunset and, unless they had made a kill,
returned before sunrise to the heavy jungle from which they
had come. By examining the sandy stretches along the bed of

this watercourse it was possible to ascertain whether a tiger had crossed into the jungle that I looked on as my private preserve, and, if so, whether it had remained or left. On the occasions on which I found only a one-way track I left the jungle severely alone and went elsewhere to look for birds.

This watercourse was of never-ending interest to me for, in addition to tigers, all the animals and all the crawling creatures that lived in the jungles that stretched for many miles on either side, crossed it, and in doing so left a photographic record of their passage. It was here, first armed with a catapult, then with a bow, later with a muzzle-loader, and later still with a modern rifle, that I added—a little at a time—to my store of jungle lore. Starting out as the sun was rising, and moving noiselessly on my bare feet, I saw at one time or another all the animals and all the crawling creatures that crossed the watercourse, until a day came when I was able to identify each by the track it made. But here was only a small beginning for I had yet to learn the habits of the animals, their language, and the part they played in the scheme of nature. And while I was accumulating knowledge of these interesting subjects I was also absorbing the language of the birds and understanding their functions in nature's garden.

The first thing I did then was to divide the birds and animals and the crawling creatures into groups. Starting with the birds, I divided them into six groups:

(a) Birds that beautified nature's garden. In this group I put minivets, orioles, and sunbirds.

(b) Birds that filled the garden with melody: thrushes, robins, and *shamas*.

(c) Birds that regenerated the garden: barbets, hornbills, and *bulbuls*.

(d) Birds that warned of danger: drongos, red jungle-fowl, and babblers.

(e) Birds that maintained the balance in nature: eagles, hawks, and owls.

(f) Birds that performed the duty of scavengers: vultures, kites, and crows.

The animals I divided into five groups:

(g) Animals that beautified nature's garden. In this group I put deer, antelope, and monkeys.

(h) Animals that helped to regenerate the garden by opening up and aerating the soil: bears, pigs and porcupines.

(i) Animals that warned of danger: deer, monkeys, and squirrels.

(j) Animals that maintained the balance in nature: tigers, leopards, and wild dogs.

(k) Animals that acted as scavengers: hyaenas, jackals, and pigs.

The crawling creatures I divided into two groups:

(l) Poisonous snakes. In this group I put cobras, kraits, and vipers.

(m) Non-poisonous snakes: Pythons, grass-snakes, and *dhamin* (rat snakes).

Having divided the principal birds and animals into groups according to the functions they performed, the other members of the jungle folk that performed similar duties were added—as my knowledge increased—to the groups to which they belonged. The next step was to make myself familiar with the language of the jungle folk, and to learn to imitate the calls of those birds and animals whose calls are within the range of human lips and of a human throat. All birds and all animals have their own language and though—with few exceptions—one species cannot speak the language of another species, all the jungle folk understand each other's language. The best three of the exceptions are, the racket-tailed drongo, the rufous-backed shrike, and the gold-fronted green *bulbul*. To bird lovers the racket-tailed drongo is a never-ending source of pleasure and interest for, in addition to being the most courageous bird in our jungles, he can imitate to perfection the calls of most birds and of one animal, the *cheetal*, and he has a great sense of humour. Attaching himself to a flock of ground-feeding birds—jungle-fowl, babblers, or thrushes—he takes up a commanding position on a dead branch and, while regaling the jungle with his own songs and the songs of the other birds, keeps a sharp look-out for enemies in the way of hawks, cats, snakes, and small boys armed with catapults, and his warning of the approach of danger is never disregarded. His services are not disinterested, for in return for protection he expects the flock he is guarding to provide him with food. His sharp eyes miss nothing, and the moment he sees that one of the birds industriously scratching up or turning over the dead leaves below him has unearthed a fat centipede or a juicy scorpion he darts at it screaming like a hawk, or screaming as a bird of the species he is trying to dispossess does when caught by a hawk. Nine times out of ten he succeeds in wresting the prize from the finder, and returning to his perch kills and eats the titbit at his leisure, and having done so continues his interrupted song.

Racket-tailed drongos are also found in association with *cheetal*, feeding on the grasshoppers and other winged insects disturbed by the deer; and having heard the *cheetal* give their alarm call on seeing a leopard or a tiger, he learns the call and repeats it with great exactitude. I was present on one occasion when a leopard killed a yearling *cheetal*. Moving the leopard away for a few hundred yards I returned to the kill and breaking down a small bush tied the kill to the stump, and as there were no suitable trees nearby I sat on the ground with my back to a bush and my cine-camera resting on my drawn-up knees. Presently a racket-tailed drongo arrived in company with a flock of white-throated laughing thrush. On catching sight of the kill the drongo came close for a better look at it and, in doing so, saw me. The kill was a natural sight to him but my presence appeared to puzzle him; however, after satisfying himself that I did not look dangerous he flew back to the white-throats who were chattering noisily on the ground. The birds were on my left and I was expecting the leopard to appear from my right front when suddenly the drongo gave the alarm call of a *cheetal*, on hearing which the white-throats—some fifty in number— rose in a body and went screaming into the branches above them, whence they started giving their alarm call. By watching the drongo I was able to follow every move of the unseen leopard who, annoyed by the baiting of the birds, worked round until he was immediately behind me. The bush in front of which I was sitting had few leaves on it, and on catching sight of me the leopard gave a low growl and retreated into the jungle, followed by the drongo. The drongo was now thoroughly enjoying himself and his rendering of the alarm call of *cheetal* filled me with admiration and with envy, for though I could have competed with him on a single call I could not have rung the changes on the different ages of the deer he was imitating as quickly or as smoothly as he was doing.

When taking up my position on the ground, I knew the leopard would see me the moment he returned to his kill, and I expected to get my picture while he was trying to take the kill away. After shaking off the drongo the leopard returned a second time and though, by growling fiercely, he showed his resentment at my presence and at the sound my camera made, I succeeded in exposing fifty feet of film—at a range of twenty yards— while he was struggling to break the creeper with which I had tied the kill to the stump.

I do not know if racket-tailed drongos can learn to talk, but I do know that they can learn to whistle tunes. Some years ago the Anglo-Indian station-master of Mankapur Junction on the Bengal and North-Western Railway, now the Oudh-Tirhut Railway, supplemented his income by teaching drongos and *shamas* to whistle tunes. Trains halted at the junction for breakfast and lunch and it was a common sight to see passengers running over to the station-master's bungalow to hear his birds, and returning with a cage containing a bird that whistled the tune they fancied most. For these birds, plus an ornate cage, the station-master charged a flat rate of thirty rupees.

chapter seven

HAVING STATED THAT THE BOOK of Nature
has no beginning and no end, I would be the
last to claim that I have learned all that is to be
learnt of any of the subjects dealt with in *Jungle
Lore*, or that the book contains any expert
knowledge. But having spent so much of my
life with nature, and having made a hobby of
jungle lore, I have observed a little knowledge,
and that knowledge I am now imparting without
reservations. I do not flatter myself that all who
read these pages will agree with my deductions
and statements, but that need be no cause for
quarrel, for no two or more people look at any
object with the same eyes. Take, for example,
three people looking at a rose. One will see only
the colour of the flower, another will see only
the shape, while the third will see both the colour
and the shape. All three will have seen what they
were looking for, and all three will have been

right. When the present Prime Minister of the United Provinces
of India and I differed on a subject under discussion, he said,
'We can agree to differ on this point, and still remain friends.'
So if any reader differs with me on any point I raise, let us
take the Prime Minister's advice and remain friends.

In the beginning I found it difficult to distinguish between
the tracks of different animals that left more or less similar
impressions on the bed of the watercourse. For instance, the
tracks of a young *sambhar* and of a young blue-bull are very
similar to the tracks of a big pig. But by watching each of these
animals crossing the watercourse and then examining its tracks
I soon found that I could, at a glance, distinguish between the
tracks of a pig and the tracks of all the other cloven-hoofed
animals in the jungle. A pig, like all deer, has rudimentary hoofs
at the back of the main hoofs. In a pig these rudimentary hoofs
are longer than they are in a deer, and except when a pig is crossing
hard ground these rudimentary
hoofs leave a distinct impression,
whereas in the case of deer the
rudimentary hoofs only leave an
impression when the main
hoofs have sunk in soft
ground. Again, until one has
gained some experience it is
difficult to tell the difference
between the pug marks of a tiger cub, and the pug marks of a
leopard, when both are of the same superficial area. The difference
between the two pug marks can be determined by looking at the
imprint of the toes, for the toes of a tiger cub are larger and out
of all proportion to the toes of a leopard when both pug marks
cover the same superficial area.

The tracks of hyaenas and those of wild dogs are often

confused with the tracks of leopards. Here—when there is any
doubt—two fundamental rules can be applied to determine the
species of the animal that has made the track:

(a) All animals that run down their prey have big toes as
    compared with their pads, and all animals that stalk their
    prey have small toes as compared with their pads.

(b) The imprint of the toe-nails shows in the tracks of all animals
    that run down their prey, and—except when startled, or
    when in the act of springing—the imprint of the claws does
    not show in the tracks of animals that stalk their prey.

If you look at the tracks of a house dog and cat, you will
see what I mean by big toes and small pads in the track of the
former, and small toes and big pads in the track of the latter.

When living in an area in which snakes are plentiful, it is
advisable on occasion to know—from its tracks—in which
direction the snake has gone and to determine, more or less
accurately, if the snake was poisonous or nonpoisonous. The girth
of a snake can also be assessed from its track. I will deal with
these three points in the order in which I have mentioned them:

(a) *Direction*: For the purpose of my illustration I should like
    you to imagine a field of closely-planted lucern, six inches
    high. If you were to run a roller across the field from right
    to left you would notice that the lucern plants were laid
    flat in the direction in which the roller had been run, so
    even if you had not been present when the roller was being
    run across the field you would have no difficulty in knowing
    that it had been run from right to left. If you are not blessed
    with good eyesight, take a magnifying glass and look carefully
    at any patch of sand or dust, and you will note that particles
    of the sand or dust stand up higher than other particles.
    Call these particles that stand upright the 'pile'. When a
    snake passes over sand or dust it lays the pile flat in the

direction in which it has gone, in the same way as the roller did with the lucern, Every surface like sand, dust, ashes, and so on, on which a snake leaves a track, has a pile on it, and remembering this, you can always tell in which direction a snake has gone by looking at the flattened pile.

(b) *Poisonous or non-poisonous*: You will note that I have said you can determine *more or less* accurately from the track of a snake whether it is poisonous or non-poisonous. There is no hard and fast rule—as in the case of direction—by which the species of a snake can be determined from its track. For though I have only seen the tracks of a few of the three hundred or more varieties of snakes in India, I know of two exceptions from the general rule I apply to determine the species from the track. The two exceptions are the hamadryad or king cobra in the case of poisonous snakes, and the python in the case of non-poisonous snakes.

Poisonous snakes, with the exception I have mentioned, lie in wait for their victims or approach them unseen. They therefore have no need for speed and move over the ground comparatively slowly, and when a snake moves slowly it can only do so by excessive wriggling. Take for example a Russell's Viper, or a krait, India's most deadly snake. If you watch one of these snakes moving over the ground, say over sand or dust, you will note that it travels in a series of short curves, and if you examine the track left by the snake, you will observe that it shows as a series of short curves. When, therefore, you see the track of a snake that shows excessive wriggling,

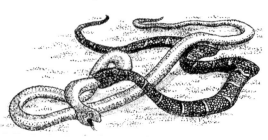

you can be reasonably sure it is the track of a poisonous snake. Hamadryads live almost exclusively on other snakes and as many of their

intended victims can move with speed, the hamadryad has
acquired a turn of speed which is said to equal that of a
horse. On this point I am ignorant for I have never chased
or been chased on horseback by this king of snakes, which
attains a length of seventeen feet. However, having killed
a few hamadryads up to fourteen feet in length, I know
they can travel fast, and this turn of speed I believe they
have acquired to enable them to catch other fast-moving
snakes. Non-poisonous snakes, with the exception I have
mentioned, are slim-built, active, and speedy; and some,
like the *dhamin* or rat snake and the black rock snake, can
cover the ground at incredible speed. Speed in non-
poisonous snakes may be essential partly to secure their
prey and partly to outstrip their enemies, of whom they
have many. When a snake covers the ground at great speed
it leaves a more or less straight track, and where there are
slight inequalities in the ground the belly of the snake only
touches the hills, and not the valleys. When, therefore, you
see a track that is comparatively straight you can be
reasonably sure it is the track of a non-poisonous snake.
The only poisonous snake whose track you might confuse
with that of a non-poisonous one is a hamadryad, but the
chances of your doing so are small, for the hamadryad is
rare and is found only in a few localities.

(c) *Girth*: To estimate the girth of a snake from the track it
makes, measure the width of the track at several points,
and multiply the mean width by four. This will give the
girth of the snake, though only approximately, for the width
of the track will depend on the surface on which it is
made. For instance, if the track is made on a light film of
dust, it will be narrower than it would be if made on
deep dust.

In India twenty thousand people die each year of snake-bite. Of these twenty thousand, I believe only half die of snake poison; the other half die of shock or fright, or a combination of the two, from the bite of non-poisonous snakes. Though Indians have lived with snakes for thousands of years it is surprising how little they know about them, and with very few exceptions Indians look upon all snakes as poisonous. The shock of a bite from a big snake is considerable, and when in addition to the shock the victim jumps to the conclusion that he has been bitten by a poisonous snake and that he is doomed, it is not surprising that such a large number of people succumb—as I believe they do—to the bite of non-poisonous snakes.

In most villages in India there are men who are credited with being able to cure people bitten by snakes. As only some ten per cent of the snakes in India are poisonous, these men build up a great reputation for themselves. They give their services free and do good work among the poor, for though they cannot with their nostrums and charms cure anyone who has received a lethal dose of snake poison, they do save the lives of many people bitten by non-poisonous snakes, by infusing them with courage and confidence.

Most hospitals in India are equipped to deal with snake-bite victims, but as the poor have no means of transport other than their own legs or the shoulders of companions, in many cases they arrive at hospital when they have passed the stage at which expert medical treatment would be of benefit to them. In all hospitals charts are exhibited of poisonous snakes. Except where rewards are paid for the destruction of poisonous snakes these charts are of little value, for most people are bitten while moving about barefoot at night, and therefore do not see the snakes that have bitten them. And again, there is a widespread belief that if the person bitten kills the snake, the snake in turn will kill him, so few snakes are produced in hospitals by snake-bite victims to enable doctors to determine whether the patient was bitten by a poisonous or a non-poisonous species.

My method—when I am in doubt—of determining whether a snake is poisonous or non-poisonous, is to kill it and look at its mouth. If it has two rows of teeth I class it as non-poisonous; while if it has two fangs on the upper jaw—hinged in the viper family and fixed in the cobra family—I class it as poisonous. A bite from the former class exhibits a number of teeth-marks; a bite from the latter class exhibits two fang-marks, though in some cases only one fang-mark, as happens occasionally when the striker is not at right angles to the object struck, or when the object struck, say a finger or a toe, is too small for both fangs to make contact.

chapter eight

LEARNING THE CALLS OF THE jungle folk
was not difficult, nor was it difficult to imitate
some of the birds and a few of the animals, for
I had a good ear, and being young my lips and
vocal chords were pliant. Learning the calls and
being able to identify every bird and animal by
its call was not sufficient, however, for, with the
exception of those birds whose function it is to
fill nature's garden with melody, birds and animals
do not call without a reason, and the call differs
according to the reason for which it is made.

I was sitting one day on a tree watching a herd
of *cheetal* in an open glade. There were fifteen
stags and hinds in the herd, and five young ones
all about the same age. One of the young ones
that had been sleeping in the sun got to its feet,
stretched itself, and kicking up its heels raced
across the glade towards a fallen tree; this was
a signal to the other young ones that a game of

'follow the leader' was on. Nose to tail the five cleared the tree, circled around, raced through the glade and again cleared the tree. After the second jump the leader carried on into the jungle beyond, followed by its companions. A hind that had been lying down now got to her feet, looked in the direction in which the young ones had gone, and gave a sharp bark. The bark brought the truants racing back to the glade, but it had not the slightest effect on the grown animals, who continued to lie down or to crop the short grass. A footpath used by woodcutters passed within a short distance of the glade and presently along this path came a man carrying an axe over his shoulder. From my raised position I saw the man while he was still a long way off, for the jungle in the direction in which he was coming was comparatively open. When the man was a hundred yards from the glade one of the hinds saw him; gave a sharp bark and the whole herd without a moment's hesitation dashed away into thick cover.

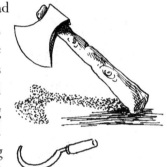

The bark of the anxious mother recalling her young one and the bark of the hind warning the herd of the presence of a human being had, to my untrained ears, sounded exactly alike and it was not until I had gained experience that I detected that the difference in the call of animals, and also of birds, when calling for different reasons was not to be found in the call itself, but in the intonation of the call. A dog barks, and all who hear it know it is barking to welcome its master; or barking with excitement at being taken for a run; or barking with frustration at a treed cat; or barking with anger at a stranger; or just barking because it is chained up. In all these cases it is the intonation of the bark that enables the hearer to determine why the dog is barking.

When I had absorbed sufficient knowledge to enable me to identify all the jungle folk by their calls, ascribe a reason for the call, and imitate many of them sufficiently well to get some birds and a few animals to come to me or to follow me, the jungles took on an added interest, for not only was I able to take an interest in the surroundings within sight but also in the surroundings to the limit of my hearing. But first it was necessary to be able to locate, or pinpoint sound. Animals who live day and night with fear can pinpoint sound with exactitude, and fear can teach human beings to do the same. Sounds that are repeated—as, for instance, a *langor* barking at a leopard, or a *cheetal* barking at a suspicious movement, or a peafowl calling at a tiger—are not difficult to locate, nor do they indicate immediate danger calling for instant action. It is the sound that is only heard once, like the snapping of a twig, a low growl, or the single warning call of bird or of animal, that is difficult to locate, is of immediate danger, and calls for instant action. Having acquired the ability—through fear—of being able to pinpoint sound, that is, to assess the exact direction and distance of all sounds heard, I was able to follow the movement of unseen leopards and tigers, whether when in the jungle by daylight, or in bed at night, for the situation of our home enabled me to hear all the jungle sounds.

In return for the birds I collected for him, Stephen Dease gave me the gun I have already referred to. This gun was a double-barrelled muzzle-loader which in its young days must have been quite a good weapon, but whose efficiency had been reduced by half by an over-charge of powder which had split the right barrel. The explosion had also evidently broken the stock, and when Stephen passed the old warrior over to me the barrels and stock were held precariously together with lappings of brass wire. However, as Kunwar Singh—my poacher friend—pointed out to me, the left barrel was sound and capable of rendering good service; a prediction that proved correct for I kept the larder for a considerable family supplied for two winters with jungle-fowl and pea-fowl, and on one memorable occasion I crept up close enough to a *cheetal* to shoot it with No. 4 shot.

I am not ashamed to admit that all the birds I shot with the muzzle-loader were shot sitting. Ammunition was not easy to come by and to eke out my scanty supply every shot had to be effective. If during a morning or an evening I fired two or three shots, I brought back two or three birds, and no other method of shooting the birds could possibly have given me more pleasure.

I was returning one evening from the foothills at the upper end of the jungle between the two watercourses I have mentioned. The weather for several weeks had been very dry, making stalking difficult, and the sun was near setting when I turned my face for home, with a jungle-fowl and a *kalege* pheasant in the string bag in which I carried my powder and shot. A blue-black cloud was showing over a shoulder of the foothills to the west as I emerged from a deep ravine in which I had shot the *kalege* pheasant. This ominous-looking cloud, following a spell of dry weather and a sultry day when not a leaf or a blade of grass had stirred, presaged a hailstorm. Hailstorms along the foothills are feared by man and beast, for in a few minutes a belt of cultivation, maybe only a quarter of a mile wide or maybe ten miles, can be laid waste and children and cattle killed if caught in the open. I have never seen a wild animal killed by hailstones, but I have seen the jungle strewn with dead birds, including vultures and peafowl.

I had three miles to go, but by taking a direct line for home and cutting the corners in the winding game-tracks I could reduce the distance by half a mile. I was now facing the oncoming blue-black cloud, across the face of which forked lightning was continuous. The birds and animals were silent and the only sound to be heard as I entered a thick belt of heavy timber was the distant rumble of thunder. Under the dense canopy of leaves the light was fading and as I loped along, taking care to see where I placed my feet for I was running barefoot, I heard the wind that always precedes a hailstorm. When I was half-way through the timber the wind struck the forest, sending the carpet of tinder-dry dead leaves swirling along the ground with the noise of a suddenly released torrent of water, and at the same moment I heard a scream—Dansay's 'banshee', without a doubt. Starting on a minor note the scream developed into a terrifying shriek, and then died away on a long-drawn-out sobbing note. Some sounds have the effect of petrifying one, others galvanize one into instant action: the scream—which I placed as being above and a little behind me—had the latter effect on me. A few weeks previously—in company with Magog—I had run from a tiger as I thought I should never run again, but I did not know then that terror of the unknown could lend wings to one's feet. To my credit be it noted that I did not throw away my gun and the heavy string bag, and regardless of thorns and of stubbed toes I ran until I reached home. Thunder was booming overhead and the first of the hailstones were hissing down as I ran up the steps of the veranda, and in the general confusion of fastening doors and windows and making all secure against the storm, my breathless and excited condition escaped attention.

Dansay had said that hearing the banshee brought calamity to the hearer and his family, and fearing that I would be blamed for any calamity that befell the family, I said not a word about my experience. Danger of any kind has an attraction for everyone, including small boys, and though for many days I avoided the area in which I had heard the banshee, a day came when I found myself back at the edge of the heavy timber. As on the evening of the storm a wind was blowing, and after I had been standing with my back to a tree for some minutes, I again heard the scream. Restraining with difficulty my impulse to run away, I stood trembling behind the tree and after the scream had been repeated a few times, I decided to creep up and have a look at the banshee. No calamity had resulted from my hearing her and I thought that if by chance she saw me now, and saw that I was a very small boy, he would not kill me; so—with my heart beating in my throat—I crept forward as slowly and as noiselessly as a shadow, until I saw Dansay's banshee.

In some violent storm of long ago a giant of the forest had been partly uprooted and had been prevented from crashing to the ground by falling across another and slightly smaller giant. The weight of the bigger tree had given the smaller tree a permanent bend, and when a gust of wind lifted the bigger one and then released it, it swayed back on to the supporting tree. At the point of impact the wood of both trees had died and worn as smooth as glass, and it was the friction between these two smooth surfaces that was emitting the terrifying scream. Not until I had laid the gun on the ground and climbed the leaning tree and sat on it while the scream was being repeated below me, was I satisfied that I had found the terror that was always at the back of my mind when I was alone in the jungles. From that day I date the desire I acquired of following up and getting to the bottom of every unusual thing I saw or heard in the jungles, and for this I am grateful to Dansay for, by frightening me with his banshee, he started me on the compiling of many exciting and interesting jungle detective stories.

Detective stories of fiction usually start with the evidence of some violent crime or attempted crime, and the enthralled reader—oblivious for the time being that he is reading fiction— is carried along through exciting scene after scene until finally the criminal is detected and made to suffer for his crime. My jungle detective stories do not start in the same way, nor do they always end with punishment for the criminal. I will select at random two of these stories from memory's library.

(1)

I was camping at a Forest Department bungalow ten miles from Kaladhungi and had gone out early one morning to try to shoot a jungle-fowl or a peafowl for the pot. To the left of the road I was on was a densely-wooded low hill with game of all kinds on it, and to the right was cultivated land with a narrow strip of bush-covered ground between the cultivation and the road. When the village folk started moving about their fields in the morning, birds that were feeding on the crops rose and flew over the road, offering excellent shots. My luck was out that morning, for the birds that crossed the road were out of range of my small bore gun, and I got to the end of the cultivation without firing a shot.

While keeping an eye open for birds, I had also kept an eye on the road, and a hundred yards from where the chances of my shooting a bird ended I noted that a big male leopard had come down the hill from my left on to the road. For a few yards the leopard had kept to the left of the road, then crossed to the right and lain down near a bush. From this point the leopard had gone forward for twenty yards, and again lain down by a bush. The behaviour of the leopard indicated that he had been interested in something, and quite evidently that something had not been on the road, for if it had he would have gone forward through the bushes and not along the road. Going back to where he had first lain I knelt down to see the view he had obtained from this spot. Where the cultivation and the narrow strip of bushes ended there was an open stretch of ground, the grass on which had been cropped close by village cattle. This stretch of ground was visible from the leopard's first viewpoint, and I found it was also visible from his second viewpoint, so what he had been interested in was evidently on the open ground.

Keeping under cover of the screen of bushes, the leopard had gone forward for another fifty yards to where the bushes ended and where a shallow depression starting at the edge of the road ran across the open ground. Where the bushes ended the leopard had lain down for some time, changing his position several times, and eventually he had entered the depression and proceeded along it, stopping and lying down frequently. Thirty yards farther on the sand and dust that had been washed off the road into the depression ended and gave place to short grass. Here, from the particles of sand and dust adhering to the grass where the leopard had put his pads, it was reasonable to assume that he passed that way after the dew had started falling the previous evening, which would be at approximately 7 p.m. The grass in the depression extended for only a few yards and the light sand and dust beyond showed no pug marks, so it was evident the leopard had left the depression at this spot. Tracking on the open ground was not possible, but from where the leopard had left the depression I saw he had gone in the direction of a few coarse tufts of grass, a foot or two high. Going up to the tufts, I saw at a distance of about ten feet the deep imprints of a *sambhar*'s hoofs. From here on for thirty yards, and at regular intervals, all four hoofs of the *sambhar* had bitten deep into the ground as would naturally happen if the *sambhar* was trying, by shock tactics, to dislodge something from his back. At the end of the thirty yards the *sambhar* had turned to the left and dashed straight towards an isolated tree on the far side of the depression. On the bark of this tree, and at a height of about four feet, I found *sambhar* hairs and a small splash of blood.

I was now convinced that the leopard from his look-out on the hill had seen the *sambhar* feeding on the open ground, and after reconnoitring the position had set off to stalk it and, having sprung on its back from the cover of the tufts of grass, that he was now riding it until it took him to some sheltered spot where he could kill it and have the kill to himself. To have killed the *sambhar* where he caught it would have been easy but he could not have dragged a full-grown *sambhar* to cover—the hoof marks had shown me that the *sambhar* was full grown—and when daylight came he would have lost his kill, so he had wisely decided to ride it. Having failed to wipe the leopard off its back on the first tree the *sambhar* made three more attempts to get rid of his unwelcome rider before making for the main jungle two hundred yards away, where he evidently hoped that bushes would accomplish what the trees had failed to do. Twenty yards inside the bushes, and well screened from the prying eyes of human beings and vultures, the leopard had buried his teeth in the old *sambhar* hind's throat, and while holding on with his teeth and the claws of his fore-paws, had swung his body clear of the hind bringing her to the ground and, after killing her, had eaten his meal. The leopard was lying near his kill when I arrived and on seeing me moved off, but he had nothing to fear from me for I was out bird shooting and was armed with a 28-bore gun and No. 8 shot.

I know of many instances of leopards riding animals they intend to kill—*sambhar*, *cheetal*, and in one instance a horse—but I only know of one instance of a tiger having done so.

On that occasion I was camped near Mangolia Khatta, a cattle station twelve miles from Kaladhungi, and while I was having a

late breakfast one morning I heard the distant boom of buffalo
bells. Earlier in the morning, while returning to camp after taking
a cinema picture of a leopard, I had passed through a herd of
some hundred and fifty buffaloes that were grazing on a wide
expanse of *tarai* grass through which ran a sandy *nullah*, with a
trickle of water in it. In this *nullah* I had seen the fresh pug
marks of a tiger and a tigress. From the violent booming of the
bells it was evident that the herd of buffaloes was stampeding
back to the cattle station, and mingled with the sound of the
bells was the bellowing of a single buffalo. The
men at the cattle station, some ten in number,
had now taken alarm and started to shout and
to beat tin cans, whereon the buffalo stopped
bellowing but the herd continued to stampede
until it reached the station.

Shortly after all the noise had died down I
heard two shots, and on going to the station to
investigate I saw a young European with a gun in
his hand and a ring of Indians standing round a
buffalo that was stretched on the ground. The
European told me that he was employed by the
Indian Wood Products at Izatnagar and that he
had been talking to the cattle men when they heard
the distant booming of the buffalo bells. As the sound
drew nearer they heard the bellowing of a buffalo and
the angry roar of a tiger (I was farther away and so had not
heard the tiger), and fearing that the tiger was coming to the
station they had started shouting and beating tin cans. On the
arrival of the herd one of the buffaloes was seen to be smothered
in blood and on the cattle men saying that nothing could be
done for it, he had asked for and obtained permission to shoot
it and had put two bullets into its head to end its suffering.

The buffalo the young man had shot was young and in perfect condition, and the cattle men were probably right when they informed me it was one of the best in the herd. I had never seen an animal in the condition it presented, so I examined it very thoroughly.

On the buffalo's neck and throat there was not a single mark of tooth or claw, but on its back were fifty or more deep cuts made by a tiger's claws. Some of these claw marks had been made while the tiger was facing towards the buffalo's head, others had been made while it had been facing towards the buffalo's tail. While riding the maddened animal the tiger had torn off and eaten some five pounds of flesh from its withers, and some ten to fifteen pounds from its hind quarters.

Going back to my camp I armed myself with a heavy rifle and went down the trail the buffaloes had made, and found that the stampede had started on the far side of the *nullah* in which I had seen the tiger's pug marks. But the grass here was unfortunately shoulder high, so I was not able to reconstruct the scene or to find any clue as to how the tiger came to be on the back of a buffalo it had no intention of killing, as was evident from the absence of marks on the buffalo's neck and throat. This failure to reconstruct the scene I greatly regret, for apart from its being the only occasion on which I have been at fault, I believe no other instance of a tiger riding an animal and having a meal while doing so has ever been known.

The pug marks in the *nullah* showed that both tigers were full grown, so it was not a case of a young and inexperienced tiger trying his hand; and, further, no young tiger would have dared to approach a herd of buffaloes at ten o'clock in the morning, or, for the matter of that, at any hour.

(2)

Evelyn Gill, son of my old friend Harry Gill, is one of the keenest butterfly collectors I know, and in a conversation I had with him while he was in Naini Tal on short leave I mentioned having seen on the Powalgarh road a butterfly with brilliant red spots on its upper wings. Evelyn said he had not seen a butterfly of this kind and he begged me to get him a specimen.

Some months later I was camped at Sandni Gaga, three miles from Powalgarh, trying to get a cinema picture of *cheetal* stags fighting, for at that time it was not unusual to see several battles between rival stags taking place at the same time on the Sandni Gaga plain. One morning after an early breakfast I set out with my butterfly net to try to get the specimen I had promised Evelyn. A hundred yards from my tent there was a forest road connecting Kaladhungi with Powalgarh, and in a hollow a mile along this road where there was a *sambhar* wallow I hoped to get the butterfly.

This forest road was little used by human beings and as there was an abundance of game in the forest through which it ran, an early morning walk along it was of great interest, for on the road, which was of hard clay with a light film of dust on it, was a record of all the animals that had used or crossed it during the night. When looking at tracks on a road or game path, with a trained eye, it is not necessary to stop at each track to determine the species, size, movement, and so on of the animal or animals that have made the track, for these details are subconsciously noted. For instance, the porcupine that had come out on to the road, a little beyond where I joined the road after leaving my camp, had evidently taken fright at something in the jungle on the right of the road and had scurried back. The reason for his fright was apparent a few yards farther on, where a bear had crossed the road from right to left. On entering the jungle on the left the bear had disturbed a sounder of pig and a small herd of *cheetal*, for they had dashed across the road into the jungle on the right. A little farther on, a *sambhar* stag had come out from the right and after browsing on a bush

had walked along the road for fifty yards, rubbed his antlers against a young sapling, and then gone back into the jungle. Near this spot a four-horned antelope, with a fawn at foot, had come on the road. The fawn, whose hoof-prints were no bigger than the finger nails of a child, had skipped about the road until the mother had taken fright, and after dashing down the road for a few yards mother and fawn had gone into the jungle. Here there was a bend in the road, and at the bend were the footprints of a hyaena who had come as far as this, and then turned and gone back the way it had come.

Reading the signs on the road and listening to the birds— Sandni Gaga in addition to being the most beautiful spot for a hundred miles round is noted for its bird life—I had covered half a mile when I came to a stretch of the road that had been cut out of the face of the hill. Here the surface was too hard to show normal tracks and I had gone a short distance along the road when my attention was arrested by an unusual mark. This was a little furrow three inches long and two inches deep where it started, and it was at right angles to the road. The furrow could have been made by a staff with an iron point, but no human being had been along the road for twenty-four hours and the furrow had been made within the past twelve hours. And again, if a human being had made it it would have been parallel with and not at right angles to the road, which at this point was fourteen feet wide with a more or less perpendicular bank some ten feet high on the right and a steep slope on the left. The earth thrown out of the furrow showed that the object that had made it had travelled from right to left.

Having satisfied myself that the furrow had not been made by a human being, I came to the conclusion that the only other thing that could have made it was the pointed tip of a horn, either of a *cheetal* or of a young *sambhar*. Had either of these deer jumped down the steep bank and made a bad landing, hard though the ground was the hoofs of the animal would have broken the surface and left a track, but there were no deer tracks anywhere near the furrow. The final conclusion that I arrived at, therefore—with the furrow as my only clue—was that it had been made by the horn of a *dead* deer, and made when a tiger had jumped down the bank with the deer in its mouth. That there were no drag marks on the road was not unusual, for whenever it is possible to do so both tigers and leopards when crossing a road with a kill lift the kill clear of the ground, and this I believe they do to avoid leaving a scent trail for bears, hyaenas, and jackals to follow.

To test the accuracy of my deductions I crossed the road and looked down the hill on the left of the road. No drag marks were to be seen, but on a bush twenty feet down the hill and at a height of about four feet I saw something glistening on a leaf in the morning sun; on going down to investigate I found this was a big drop of blood, not yet quite dry. From here on, tracking was easy, and fifty yards farther down under the shelter of a small tree and surrounded by thick bushes I found the kill, a *cheetal* stag with horns that many a sportsman would have prized as a good trophy. The tiger was taking no chances of his kill—from which he had eaten both hind quarters—being found by bird or beast, for he had scratched together the dry leaves and twigs for a considerable distance round, and had heaped them on the kill. When a tiger does this it is an indication that he is not lying up nearby to keep an eye on the kill.

I had been told by Fred Anderson and Huish Edye of a big tiger in this area which Mrs (now Lady) Anderson had christened the Bachelor of Powalgarh. I had long wished to see this famous tiger that all the sportsmen in the province were trying to bag, and which I knew lived in a deep ravine that started near the *sambhar* wallow I was making for. As there were no pug marks near the kill by which I could identify the tiger that had killed the *cheetal*, it occurred to me that it was just possible that the kill was the property of the Bachelor and, if so, that there was now a reasonable chance of my having a look at this tiger to see if he was as big as he was reputed to be.

Starting from near the kill a narrow glade ran down to a small stream a hundred yards away. Beyond the stream was a dense patch of wild lime. If the Bachelor had not gone back to his ravine he would in all probability be lying up in this patch of cover, so I decided to try to get the tiger to return to his kill. Having come to this decision I went up towards the road and buried my white butterfly net under dead leaves. The glade at the upper end was about ten feet wide and the tree under which the kill was lying was about the same distance from the right-hand side of the glade. On the left-hand side, and nearly opposite the kill was the dead stump of a tree roofed over with

creepers. First seeing that there were no holes in the dead stump
to harbour snakes, I cleared away the dry leaves from the foot
of the stump—to avoid sitting on scorpions—and then made
myself comfortable with my back to the stump. From my seat
I could see the kill, which was about thirty feet away, and I
could also see down the glade to the stream, on the far side of
which a troupe of red monkeys were feeding on the berries of
a *pipal* tree.

When my preparations were completed, I gave the call of a
leopard. Leopards will—when it is safe for them to do so—eat
a tiger's kill, and of this tigers are very resentful. If the tiger
was within hearing distance, and if my imitation was sufficiently
good to deceive him, I expected him to come up the glade, and
after I had had a good look at him I intended letting him know
I was there and then make my getaway. The monkeys responded
to my call by giving their alarm call, and three of them took up
positions on a branch that jutted out from the *pipal* tree at right

angles at a height of about
forty feet above ground.
The alarm call of the
monkeys which, as they
could not see me, only
lasted for a minute or so
was all to the good, for if
the tiger was in the vicinity
he would now be assured

that a leopard was interfering with his kill. I kept my eye on
the three monkeys, and presently I saw one of them turn round,
peer into the jungle behind him, bob his head up and down
several times, and then he gave an alarm call. A minute later
the other two started calling and were followed by several others
farther up the tree. The tiger was coming, and I greatly regretted

not having my camera with me for he would make a grand picture, walking up the glade with the sun glinting on the water of the stream and the *pipal* tree with the excited monkeys on it in the background.

As usually happens on these occasions, however, the tiger did not do what I expected. After a long pause, during which I had the uneasy feeling that the tiger was approaching his kill from behind me, I caught a fleeting glimpse of him as he sprang across the stream and disappeared into the thick jungle on the right-hand side of the glade. After reconnoitring the position from the bushes beyond the stream the tiger had evidently concluded that if he came up the glade the leopard would see him, so he had started out to stalk the kill where he evidently expected to find the leopard. As far as I was concerned there was no objection to his doing this, though it would mean his coming closer to me than I had intended letting him.

The ground was carpeted with dry leaves, and the tiger accomplished his stalk without my hearing a sound. I next saw him as he was standing looking down at his kill but, to my great unease, I found I was not looking at the Bachelor, but at a big tigress. At the best of times a tigress's temper cannot be relied on, and this was not one of those 'best of times', for I was sitting too close to her kill for my comfort, and , further it was quite possible that she had cubs in the lime thicket, in which case she would resent my presence near her kill. However, if she went back the way she had come all would be well, but the tigress did not do this. After satisfying herself that the leopard had not touched her kill, she walked out on to the glade, halving the distance between us. For a long minute she stood undecided, while I held my breath and closed my eyes until I was looking through a slit, and then she quietly walked down the glade, lay down at the stream, had a drink, and then sprang across the stream and disappeared into the thick cover.

In both the incidents I have related in these stories I did not know, at the start, that a crime had been committed, and it is this uncertainty of not knowing what a small clue will lead up to that makes the compiling of jungle detective stories so interesting and so exciting.

Few can compile a detective story of fiction, but all can compile jungle detective stories provided they have eyes to see more than the road they walk on, and provided also that they do not start with the assumption that they know all, before in fact they know anything.

chapter nine

WHEN I WAS TEN YEARS of age I was
considered old enough to join the school cadet
company of the Naini Tal Volunteer Rifles.
Volunteering was very popular and was taken
very seriously in India in those days, and all
able-bodied boys and men took pride and
pleasure in joining the force. There were four
cadet companies and one adult company in our
battalion with a combined strength of 500 which,
for a population of 6,000, meant that every one
in twelve was a volunteer.

The Principal of our school of seventy boys
was also captain of the school cadet company,
which mustered fifty strong. The holder of these
dual posts was an ex-army man and it was his
burning, and very praiseworthy, ambition to have
the best cadet company in the battalion and to
satisfy this ambition we small boys suffered, and
suffered greatly. Twice a week we drilled on the

school playground, and once a week we drilled with the other four companies on the flats, an open stretch of ground at the upper end of the Naini Tal lake.

Our captain never missed, nor did he ever overlook a fault, and all mistakes made on the drill grounds were atoned for after evening school. Taking up a position four feet from his target and wielding a four-foot-long cane, the captain was a marksman of repute who had earned for himself the title of 'Dead Eye Dick'. I do not know if he made private bets with himself, but we small boys laid wagers of marbles, tops, pen-knives, and even on occasions the biscuit that formed our breakfast, that nine times out of ten our captain could lay his cane along the most painful weal left on the hand by the previous day's or previous week's caning, and the boy—usually a newcomer—who betted against the odds always lost. The cadets of the other three companies hotly disputed our reputation of being the best drilled company, but they did not dispute our claim of our being the best turned-out company. This claim was justified, for before being marched down to drill with the other companies we were subjected to an inspection that detected the minutest particle of dirt under a finger-nail, or speck of dust on the uniform.

Our uniforms—passed down when grown out of—were of dark blue serge of a quality guaranteed to stand hard wear and to chafe every tender part of the skin they came in contact with, and, further, to show every speck of dust. Hot and uncomfortable as the uniform was it was surpassed in discomfort by the helmet that was worn with it. Made of some heavy compressed material, this instrument of torture was armed with a four-inch-long fluted metal spike, the threaded butt end of which projected down inside the helmet for an inch or more. To keep the threaded end from boring into the brain the inner band had to

be lined with paper, and when the helmet had been fixed to
the head like a vice it was held in that position by a heavy
metal chin strap mounted on hard leather. After three hours in
the hot sun few of us left the drill ground without a splitting
headache which made repetition of lessons prepared the previous
night difficult, with the result that the four-foot cane was used
more freely on drill days than on any other.

On one of our drill days on the flats the battalion was inspected
by a visiting officer of senior rank. After an hour of musketry
drill and marching and counter-marching, the battalion was
marched up to the Suka Tal (dry lake) rifle range. Here the cadet
companies were made to sit down on the hillside while the
adult company demonstrated to the visiting officer their prowess
with the 450 Martini rifle. The battalion prided itself on having
some of the best rifle shots in India in its ranks, and this pride
was reflected in every member of the force. The target, standing
on a masonry platform, was made of heavy sheet-iron and the
experts could tell from the ring of the bullet on the iron sheet
whether it had struck the centre of the target or the edge of it.

Each cadet company had its hero in the adult company, and
adverse comments against the marksmanship of a selected hero
would that morning have resulted in many sanguinary fights,
had fighting in uniform not been frowned on. After the scores
of the best shots had been announced, the cadets were ordered
to fall in and march down from the five-hundred- to the two-
hundred-yard range. Here four senior cadets were selected from
each company and we juniors were ordered to pile arms and
sit down behind the firing point.

Inter-school competition in all forms of sport, and most of
all on the rifle range, was very keen and every shot fired that
morning by the four competing teams was eagerly watched and
fiercely commented on by friend and foe alike. The scores ran

close, for the best shots in each company had been selected by the respective company commanders, and there was great jubilation in our ranks when it was announced that our team had come out second in the competition and that we had been beaten by only one point by the school that had three times our membership.

While we—the rank and file—were commenting on the achievements of the recent competitors, the Sergeant-Major was seen to detach himself from the group of officers and instructors standing at the firing point, and come towards us bellowing in a voice that it was claimed could be heard a mile away, 'Corbett, Cadet Corbett!' Heavens! What had I done now that merited punishment? True I had said that the last shot that had put the rival company one point ahead of us had been a fluke, and someone had offered to fight me, but there had been no fight for I did not even know who the challenger was, and here now was that awful Sergeant-Major again bellowing, 'Corbett, Cadet Corbett!' 'Go on.' 'He's calling you.' 'Hurry up or you'll catch it,' was being said on all sides of me; and at last, in a very weak voice, I answered 'Yes sir.' 'Why didn't you answer? Where is your carbine? Fetch it at once,' were rapped out at me all in one breath. Dazed by these commands I stood undecided until a push from behind by a friendly hand and an urgent 'Go on you fool' set me off at a run for my carbine.

On our arrival at the two-hundred-yard range those of us who were not competing had been made to pile arms, and my carbine had been used to lock one of the piles. In my effort now to release my carbine the whole pile of arms clattered to the ground and while I was trying to set the pile up again the Sergeant-Major yelled, 'Leave those carbines you have mucked up alone, and bring yours here.' 'Shoulder arms, right turn, quick march', were the next orders I received. Feeling far worse than any lamb could possibly ever have felt I was led off to the firing point, the Sergeant-Major whispering over his shoulder as we started, 'Don't you dare disgrace me.'

At the firing point the visiting officer asked if I was the youngest cadet in the battalion, and on being told that I was, he said he would like to see me fire a few rounds. The way in which this was said—and the kindly smile that went with it— gave me the feeling that of all the officers and instructors who were standing round, the visiting officer was the only one who realized how alone, and how nervous, a small boy suddenly called upon to perform before a large and imposing gathering can feel.

The 450 Martini carbine the cadets were armed with had the most vicious kick of any small-arms weapon ever made, and the musketry course I had recently been put through had left my shoulder—which was not padded with overmuch flesh— very tender and very painful, and the knowledge that it would now be subjected to further kicks added to my nervousness. However, I would have to go through with it now, and suffer for being the youngest cadet. So on the command of the Sergeant- Major I lay down, picked up one of the five rounds that had been laid down for me, loaded the carbine and raising it very gently to my shoulder took what aim I could and pressed the trigger. No welcome ring came to my anxious ears from the iron target, only a dull thud, and then a quiet voice said, 'All right, Sergeant-Major, I will take over now,' and the visiting officer, in his spotless uniform, came and lay down beside me on the oily drugget. 'Let me have a look at your carbine,' he said, and when I passed it over to him a steady hand carefully adjusted the back-sight to two hundred yards, a detail I had omitted to attend to. The carbine was then handed back to me with the injunction to take my time, and each of the following four shots brought a ring from the target. Patting me on the shoulder the visiting officer got to his feet and asked what score I had made and on being told that I had made ten, out of a possible twenty, with the first shot a miss he said, 'Splendid. Very good shooting indeed,' and as he turned to speak to the officers and instructors I went back to my companions, walking on air. But my elation was short lived, for I was greeted with, 'Rotten shot.' 'Disgraced the Company.' 'Could have done better with my eyes closed.' 'Crumbs, did you see that first shot, went and hit the hundred-yard firing point.' Boys are like that. They just speak their minds without any thought or intention of being cruel or unkind.

The visiting officer who befriended me that day on the Suka Tal rifle range when I was feeling lonely and nervous, later became the nation's hero and ended his career as Field-Marshal Earl Roberts. When I have been tempted, as many times I have been, to hurry over a shot or over a decision, the memory of that quiet voice telling me to take my time has restrained me and I have never ceased being grateful to the great soldier who gave me that advice.

The Sergeant-Major who for many years ruled the Naini Tal Volunteers with a rod of iron, was short and fat with a neck like a bull's and a heart of gold. After our last drill on the flats that term he asked me if I would like to have a rifle. Surprise and delight rendered me speechless; however, no reply appeared to be expected, and he went on to say, 'Come and see me before you leave for the holidays and I will give you a service rifle and all the ammunition you want, provided you promise to keep the rifle clean, and to return me the empties.'

So that winter I went down to Kaladhungi armed with a rifle, and without any anxiety about ammunition. The rifle the good Sergeant-Major had selected for me was dead accurate, and though a 450 rifle firing a heavy bullet may not have been the best type of weapon for a boy to train on, it served my purpose. The bow and arrow had enabled me to penetrate farther into the jungles than the catapult, and the muzzle-loader had enabled me to penetrate farther than the bow and arrow; and now, armed with a rifle, the jungles were open to me to wander in wherever I chose to go.

Fear stimulates the senses of animals, keeps them 'on their toes', and adds zest to the joy of life; fear can do the same for human beings. Fear had taught me to move noiselessly, to climb trees, to pin-point sound; and now, in order to penetrate into the deepest recesses of the jungle and enjoy the best in nature, it was essential to learn how to use my eyes, and how to use my rifle.

A human being has a field of vision of 180 degrees, and when in a jungle in which all forms of life are to be met with, including poisonous snakes and animals that have been wounded by others, it is necessary to train the eyes to cover the entire field of vision. Movements straight in front are easy to detect and easy to deal with, but movements at the edge of the field of vision are vague and indistinct and it is these vague and indistinct movements that can be most dangerous, and are most to be feared. Nothing in the jungle is deliberately aggressive, but circumstances may arise to make some creature so, and it is against the possibility of these chance happenings that the eye must be trained. On one occasion the darting in and out of the forked tongue of a cobra in a hollow tree, and on another occasion the moving of the tip of the tail of a wounded leopard lying behind a bush, warned me just in time that the cobra was on the point of striking and the leopard on the point of springing. On both these occasions I had been looking straight in front, and the movements had taken place at the extreme edge of my field of vision.

The muzzle-loader had taught me to economize ammunition and now, when I had a rifle, I considered it wasteful to practise on a fixed target, so I practised on jungle-fowl and on peafowl, and I can recall only one instance of having spoilt a bird for the table. I never grudged the time spent, or the trouble taken, in stalking a bird and getting a shot, and when I attained sufficient accuracy with the rifle to place the heavy 450 bullet exactly where I wanted to, I gained confidence to hunt in those areas of the jungle into which I previously been too frightened to go.

One of these areas, known to the family as the Farm Yard, was a dense patch of tree and scrub jungle several miles in extent, and reputed to be 'crawling' with jungle-fowl and tigers. Crawling was not an overstatement as far as the jungle-fowl were concerned, for nowhere have I seen these birds in greater numbers than in those days in the Farm Yard. The Kota-Kaladhungi road runs for a part of its length through the Farm Yard and it was on this road that the old dak runner, some years later, told me he had seen the pug marks of the 'Bachelor of Powalgarh'.

I had skirted round the Farm Yard in the bow-and-arrow and muzzle-loader days, but it was not until I was armed with the 450 that I was able to muster sufficient courage to explore this dense tree and scrub jungle. Through the jungle ran a deep and narrow ravine, and up this ravine I was going one evening intent on shooting a bird for the pot, or a pig for our villagers, when I heard jungle-fowl scratching among the dead leaves in the jungle to my right. Climbing on to a rock in the ravine I sat down, and on cautiously raising my head above the bank saw some twenty to thirty jungle-fowl feeding towards me, led by

an old cock in full plumage. Selecting the cock for my target, I
was waiting with finger on trigger for his head to come in line
with a tree—I never fired at a bird until I had a solid background
for the bullet to go into—when I heard a heavy animal on the
left of the ravine and on turning my head I saw a big leopard
bounding down the hill straight towards me. The Kota road
here ran across the hill, two hundred yards above me, and quite
evidently the leopard had taken fright at something on the road
and was now making for shelter as fast as he could go. The
jungle-fowl had also seen the leopard and as they rose with a
great flutter of wings, I slewed round on the rock to face the
leopard. Failing in the general confusion to see my movement
the leopard came straight on, pulling up when he arrived at the
very edge of the ravine.

The ravine here was about fifteen feet wide with steep banks
twelve feet high on the left, and eight feet high on the right.
Near the right bank, and two feet lower than it, was the rock
on which I was sitting; the leopard was, therefore, a little above,
and the width of the ravine from me. When he pulled up at

the edge of the ravine he turned his head to look back the way
he had come, thus giving me an opportunity of raising the rifle
to my shoulder without the movement being seen by him. Taking
careful aim at his chest I pressed the trigger just as he was turning
his head to look in my direction. A cloud of smoke from the
black-powder cartridge obscured my view and I only caught a
fleeting glimpse of the leopard as he passed over my head and
landed on the bank behind me, leaving splashes of blood on
the rock on which I was sitting, and on my clothes.

With perfect confidence in the rifle, and in my ability to
put a bullet exactly where I wanted to, I had counted on killing
the leopard outright and was greatly disconcerted now to find
that I had only wounded him. That the leopard was badly

wounded I could see from the blood, but I lacked the experience
to know—from the position of the wound, and the blood—
whether the wound was likely to prove fatal or not. Fearing that
if I did not follow him immediately he might get away into some
inaccessible cave or thicket where it would be impossible for
me to find him, I reloaded the rifle and stepping from my rock
on to the bank, set off to follow the blood trail.

For a hundred yards the ground was flat, with a few scattered
trees and bushes, and beyond this it fell steeply away for fifty
yards before again flattening out. On this steep hillside there
were many bushes and big rocks, behind any one of which the
leopard might have been sheltering. Moving with the utmost
caution, and scanning every foot of ground, I had gone half-

way down the hillside when from behind a rock, some twenty yards away, I saw the leopard's tail and one hind leg projecting. Not knowing whether the leopard was alive or dead I stood stock still until presently the leg was withdrawn, leaving only the tail visible. The leopard was alive and to get a shot at him I would have to move either to the right or to the left. Having already hit the leopard in the body, and not killed him, I now decided to try his head, so inch by inch I crept to the left until his head came into view. He was lying with his back to the rock, looking away from me. I had not made a sound but the leopard appeared to sense that I was near, and as he was turning his head to look at me I put a bullet into his ear. The range was short, and I had taken my time, and I knew now that the leopard was dead, so going up to him I caught him by the tail and pulled him away from the blood in which he was lying.

It is not possible for me to describe my feelings as I stood looking down at my first leopard. My hands had been steady from the moment I first saw him bounding down the steep hillside and until I pulled him aside to prevent the blood from staining his skin. But now, not only my hands but my whole body was trembling: trembling with fear at the thought of what would have happened if, instead of landing on the bank behind me, the leopard had landed on my head. Trembling with joy at the beautiful animal I had shot, and trembling most of all with anticipation of the pleasure I would have in carrying the news of my great success to those at home who I knew would be as pleased and as proud of my achievement as I was. I could have screamed, shouted, danced, and sung, all at one and the same time. But I did none of these things, I only stood and trembled, for my feelings were too intense to be given expression in the jungle, and could only be relieved by being shared with others.

I had no idea how heavy a leopard was, but I was determined to carry my leopard home; so, laying the rifle down, I ran back

to the ravine where there was a bauhinia creeper, and stripping
off sufficient of the inner bark to make a strong rope, I returned
and tied the fore and the hind legs of the leopard together. Then
squatting down I got the legs across my shoulders but found I
could not stand up, so I dragged the leopard on to the rock
and again tried and found I could not lift it. Realizing that the
leopard would have to be left, I hastily broke some branches
and, covering it up, set off on my three-mile run for home. There
was great excitement and great rejoicing in the home when I
arrived with the news that I had shot a leopard, and within a
few minutes Maggie and I, accompanied by two hefty servants,
were on our way to the Farm Yard to bring home my first leopard.

It is fortunate that Providence does not exact retribution
for the mistakes of beginners or my first encounter with a leopard
would probably have been my last, for I made the mistake of
shooting at that first leopard when it was above and within
springing distance of me, without knowing where to hit it to
kill it outright. My total bag of animals up to that date was one
cheetal—shot with the muzzle-loader—and three pigs and one
kakar, shot with the 450 rifle. The pigs and the *kakar* I killed
stone dead, and I thought I could also kill the leopard stone
dead by shooting it in the chest, and there I made my mistake.
For I learnt subsequently that though a leopard can be killed
stone dead, it is seldom possible to do this by shooting it in
the chest.

When a leopard receives a body wound that does not kill it
outright or disable it, it springs wildly, and though leopards
never attack deliberately immediately on being shot at, there is
always a risk of their making accidental contact with the
sportsman, especially when they are above and within springing
distance, and this risk is increased when the wounded animal
is not aware of the position of its assailant. That the leopard in
his wild spring landed on the bank behind me and not on my

head was my good fortune, for not knowing where I was he might have made accidental contact with me, which would have been just as unpleasant as a deliberate attack.

As an example of how uncertain a chest shot is, I will relate another experience I had with a leopard I shot in the chest. Maggie and I were camped one winter at Mangolia Khatta, a cattle station to which the animals of our village were sent when grazing in the Kaladhungi jungles became scarce. One morning while we were having breakfast the barking of a herd of *cheetal* apprised me of the fact that one of their number had been killed by a leopard. I had gone to Mangolia Khatta to try to shoot a leopard that was taking toll of our cows, and as there appeared to be a chance of getting a shot at the leopard now, I left Maggie to finish her breakfast and, picking up a 275 rifle, set off to investigate.

The deer were calling four hundred yards due west of us, but to get to them I had to make a detour to avoid an impenetrable canebrake and swampy ground. Approaching the calling animals from the south, with the wind in my face, I saw some fifty stags and hinds standing on an open patch of burnt ground and looking in the direction of the canebrake. On the swampy ground between the canebrake and the open ground there was a belt of grass some two hundred yards wide, and from the open ground, and at a distance of sixty yards from me, a leopard was attempting to drag a *cheetal* stag towards this belt of grass. It was not possible to approach any nearer to the leopard without being seen by the herd of *cheetal*, who would have warned the leopard of my presence, so I sat down and raising my rifle waited for the leopard to give me a shot.

The stag was big and heavy and the leopard was having great difficulty in dragging it over the rough ground, and presently it released its hold and stood up facing me. A leopard's white chest, flecked with black, is a perfect target for an accurate rifle at sixty yards, and when I pressed the trigger I knew I had put the bullet where I wanted to. On receiving my shot the leopard sprang high into the air, and landing on all fours, dashed into the belt of grass. Going to the spot where the leopard had been standing I saw a blood trail leading to the grass, which here was

about waist-high. Breaking some branches off a nearby tree, I covered up the stag to prevent vultures getting at it, for the stag was in velvet and in prime condition and I knew our men would be glad to have it. Returning to camp I finished my breakfast and then, accompanied by four of our tenants, went back to recover the stag and to follow up the wounded leopard. As we approached the spot from where I had fired, one of the men touched me on the shoulder and pointed to our right front, where the burnt ground ended and the belt of grass began. After a little while I saw what he was pointing at. It was a leopard, two hundred and fifty yards away, standing near the edge of the belt of grass.

Our tenants, when in camp with us, stoutly refuse to accept any payment for their services, but when out in the jungles we compete among ourselves to see who will be the first to spot a shootable animal, and when I lose they accept with great glee the rupee I pay as forfeit. When I had paid my forfeit to the two men who claimed to have seen the leopard at the same time, I told them to sit down for the leopard had now turned and was coming in our direction. Quite evidently this was the mate of the one I had wounded and, attracted to the spot as I had been, was coming to see what its mate had killed. A hundred yards from us a tongue of grass extended for a few yards on to the open ground, and on reaching this spot—from where the leopard could see the kill—it stopped for several minutes, offering me a shot at its chest, but as I already had one leopard with a chest wound on my hands I held my fire.

The leopard was very suspicious of the branches I had heaped on the kill; however, after a careful look all round, it cautiously approached the kill and as it stood broadside on to me I put a bullet into it an inch or two behind the left shoulder. It fell at my shot and did not move again and on going up to it I found it was dead. Telling the men to tie it to the bamboo pole they had brought and carry it to camp and return for the stag, I set out on the very unpleasant task of following up a wounded leopard in waist-high grass.

The unwritten law that a wounded animal must be recovered at all costs is accepted by all sportsmen and—where carnivora are concerned—each individual has his own method of accomplishing this end. Those who have the command of elephants find the task an easy one, but those like myself who shoot on foot have to learn by experience the best method of putting wounded carnivora out of their suffering, and avoiding injury while doing so. Burning a jungle to recover a wounded animal is, in my opinion, both cruel and wasteful, for if the animal is able to move the chances are that it will get away to die, maybe days or weeks later, and if it is too badly wounded to move there is a certainty of its being roasted alive.

It is not possible to follow the blood trail of carnivora in high grass with any degree of safety, and the method I adopted on the occasions on which I retrieved wounded carnivora in grass was to ignore the blood trail and to proceed inch by inch in the direction in which the animal had gone, hoping for the

best while prepared for the worst. On hearing the slightest sound
a wounded animal will either charge or betray its position by
some movement. If a charge does not materialize and the looked-
for movement is observed, a stone or a billet of wood, or even
a hat, can be usefully used and the animal dealt with when it
charges at the thrown object. This method can only be adopted
when there is no wind to rustle the grass, and when the sportsman
has had some experience of shooting in grass, for though wounded
carnivora are very vocal when disturbed they keep close to the
ground and seldom show themselves until the last moment.

There was no wind of any account that day at Mangolia
Khatta, and after leaving my men I followed the blood trail
over the burnt ground to where it entered the grass. Satisfying
myself that my rifle was loaded and that it was working smoothly,
I stepped very cautiously into the grass, and as I did so I heard
a whistle behind me and on looking round saw my men
beckoning to me. On my rejoining them they pointed to three

bullet holes they had found in the dead leopard while tying it to the bamboo pole. One was the bullet hole behind the left shoulder that had killed the leopard; of the other two, one was in the centre of the chest, while the other—an exit hole—was two inches from the root of the tail.

The leopard, I very greatly regret to say, had a reason for returning to its kill, and when I found what this reason was I was consumed with remorse. Leopard cubs can fend for themselves at a very young age by catching small birds, rats, mice, and frogs, and I can only hope that the cubs of the gallant mother, who after being wounded, risked her life to procure food for her young, were old enough to fend for themselves, for all my efforts to find them failed.

My statement that before entering the grass to follow up the wounded leopard, I satisfied myself that my rifle was loaded and working smoothly, will appear unusual to sportsmen in view of the fact that I had a minute previously walked up to a leopard I had just shot, and presumably I had not done so with an empty rifle without knowing whether the leopard was alive or dead. What necessity then was there for me to *satisfy* myself that my rifle was loaded? I will tell why I did so, not only on this occasion but on every occasion on which my life has depended on my rifle being loaded. Fortunately I learnt my lesson when I was comparatively young, and to this I attribute the fact that I have lived to tell the tale.

Shortly after starting work at Mokameh Ghat, of which I have told in *My India*, I invited two friends to shoot with me at Kaladhungi. Both men, Silver and Mann, had recently arrived in India and had never fired a shot in the jungles. The morning after their arrival I took them out, and two miles along the Haldwani road I heard a leopard killing a *cheetal* in the jungle to the right of the road. Knowing it would not be possible for my friends to stalk the leopard, I decided to put one of them up on a tree over the kill, and told them to draw lots. Silver was armed with a ·500 D.B. rifle which he had borrowed, while Mann was armed with a 400 S.B. black-powder rifle, also borrowed. I was armed with a ·275 magazine rifle. As Silver was a little older, and better armed than Mann, Mann very sportingly declined to draw, and the three of us set off to find the kill. The *cheetal*, a fine stag, was still twitching when we found it, and selecting a tree for Silver to sit on I left Mann to help him up, while I moved the leopard away to prevent it seeing Silver climbing the tree. The leopard was very hungry and disinclined to move; however, by zigzagging in front of him I drove him away and then returned to the kill. Silver had never before climbed a tree and was looking very unhappy, and I am not sure that I cheered him by remarking that the leopard was a big male, and cautioning him to be very careful over his shot. Then telling him that he would only have to wait a matter of five minutes, I took Mann away.

A hundred yards from the kill there was a fire track that met the Haldwani road at right angles. Going through the jungles to this track, Mann and I had only proceeded a short distance along it when Silver fired two shots in quick succession, and as we turned round to retrace our steps we saw the leopard dashing across the track. Silver did not know whether he had hit the leopard or not, but on going to the spot where Mann and I had seen it crossing the track we found a blood trail. Telling my companions to sit on the track and wait for me, I set off alone to deal with the leopard. There was nothing heroic in this, quite the contrary in fact, for when following wounded carnivora it is necessary to concentrate attention on the matter in hand and it is difficult to do this when accompanied by companions with fingers on the triggers of cocked rifles. When I had gone

a short distance Silver came after me and offered to accompany
me, and when I declined his offer he begged me to take his rifle,
saying he would never forgive himself if the leopard attacked
me and I was unable to defend myself with my light rifle. So,
to please him, we exchanged rifles. As Silver walked back to
the fire track I set off for the second time, but before doing so
I uncocked his rifle and opened the breach sufficiently to see
that there were two cartridges in the chambers.

The ground for a hundred yards was comparatively open,
and then the blood trail led into heavy cover. As I approached
this cover I heard the leopard moving in front of me, and for a
second I thought it was on the point of charging. The sound
was not repeated, however, so very cautiously I entered the
cover and twenty yards farther on found where the leopard had
been lying, and from where he had got up when I heard him.
It was now a case of moving step by step and I was thankful,
when a hundred and fifty yards farther on, the trail led out on
to more open ground. There I was able to move faster and I
had covered another hundred yards when, on approaching a
big *haldu* tree, I caught sight of the tip of the leopard's tail
projecting from the right-hand side of the tree. Finding he was
being followed the leopard had quite evidently taken up what
he considered would be the best position for his charge, and
that he would charge I had no doubt whatever.

Deciding it would be to my advantage to meet a head-on
charge, I moved to the left of the tree. As the leopard's head
came into view I saw he was lying flat down, facing me, with his
chin resting on his outstretched paws. His eyes were open, and
the tips of his ears and his whiskers were trembling. The leopard
should have sprung at me the moment I appeared round the
tree, and that he had not done so made me hold my fire, for it
had not been my intention to blow his head off at a range of a

few feet, but to put a bullet into his body and so avoid ruining Silver's trophy. As I continued to stare at him his eyes closed and I realized that he was dead, that in fact he had died as I was watching him. To make sure I was right I coughed and as there was no response, I picked up a stone and hit him on the head.

Silver and Mann came up at my call and before handing Silver's rifle back to him I opened the breach and extracted the two brass cartridges, and, to my horror, found that both were empty. Many sportsmen have suffered through pulling the triggers of empty rifles, and had I not been slowed down while following the blood trail through heavy cover, I would have added to the number. From the day I learnt my lesson, fortunately without injury to myself, I have never approached dangerous ground without satisfying myself that the weapon I am carrying is loaded. If I am carrying a double-barrelled rifle I change the cartridges from one chamber to the other, and if I am carrying a single-barrelled rifle I eject the cartridge, see that the bolt is working smoothly, and then replace the cartridge in the chamber.

chapter ten

KUNWAR SINGH, OF WHOM I wrote in *My India*, had a great aversion to shooting in the jungles near Kaladhungi, which he said were full of ground creepers which made it difficult to run away from zealous forest guards and angry tigers, and for this reason he confined all his poaching activities to the Garuppu jungles. Good woodsman and good shot though he was, and greatly as I admired him, Kunwar Singh was not a super-sportsman and this I attribute to the fact that the jungles in which he did his shooting were teeming with game. Knowing every game-path and every glade and open stretch of ground on which deer were to be found, his method of approach was to stride through the jungles without any attempt at silence, and if he disturbed the deer in one glade he would say it did not matter for there were sure to be more in the next glade. Nevertheless I learnt many things from Kunwar Singh for which I have never ceased to be grateful, and I am also grateful to him for having helped me to overcome some of my fears of the unknown. One of these fears concerned forest fires. Having heard of the danger of forest fires and seen the effect of them in our jungles, I carried the fear in the back of my mind that I would one day be caught by a forest fire and roasted alive, and it was Kunwar Singh who dispelled this fear.

In village areas in the Kumaon foothills every one is interested in his neighbour's affairs or doings, and to people who never see a daily paper and whose lives are, more or less, circumscribed by the forest that surrounds their village or group of villages, every scrap of news is of interest and is eagerly passed on, losing nothing in repetition. It was not surprising, therefore, for Kunwar Singh to have heard about my shooting of the leopard in the Farm Yard almost before the animal had time to cool, and being the sportsman he was he lost no time in coming to congratulate me. He knew about the rifle the Sergeant-Major had lent me, but until I shot the leopard I do not think he had any faith in my ability to use it. Now, however, with this concrete evidence before him he evinced a great interest in me and in the rifle, and before he left me that day I had promised to meet him at 5 o'clock on the following morning at the fourth milestone on the Garuppu road.

It was pitch dark when Maggie brewed a cup of tea for me, and with an hour in hand I set off to keep my appointment with Kunwar Singh. I had walked that lonely forest road on many occasions and the dark held no terror for me, and as I approached the fourth milestone I saw the glimmer of a fire under a tree by the side of the road. Kunwar Singh had arrived before me and as I sat down near his fire to warm my hands he said, 'Oh look, you have come away in such a hurry that you have forgotten to put on your trousers.' I tried, with little success, to convince

Kunwar Singh that I had not forgotten to don my trousers but that I was wearing—for the first time—a new style of nether garment called shorts. For though he confined himself to saying that *jangias* (panties) were not suitable for the jungles, his look implied that I was indecently clothed and that he would be hanged if he would be seen with me in public. After this bad start the atmosphere did not clear until a jungle-cock started crowing in a near-by tree, on hearing which Kunwar Singh got to his feet, put out the fire, and said it was time to be going for we still had a long way to go.

The jungle was awakening as we left our tree and stepped out on the road. The jungle-cock who, awakened by our fire, had crowed his welcome to the coming day had set a sound wave in motion and each bird, big and small, as it roused from slumber added its voice to the growing volume of sound. Though our jungle-cock is the first bird to rub the sleep from his eyes, he is not the first to descend to the ground. The privilege of catching the early worm is claimed by the Himalayan whistling-thrush, better known as the whistling-schoolboy. While walking through the Kumaon jungles in the half-light between day and night, or night and day, a bird will flit by on silent wings pouring out a stream of golden song which once heard will never be forgotten. The songster is the whistling schoolboy bidding the closing day good night, or welcoming the new-born day. Morning and evening he pours out his song while in flight, and during the day he sits for hours in a leafy tree whistling in a soft sweet minor key a song that has no beginning and no end. Next to greet the coming light is the racket-tailed drongo and a minute later he is followed by the peafowl. No one may sleep after the peafowl has given his piercing call from the topmost branch of the giant *samal* tree and now, as night dies and daylight comes, a thousand throbbing throats in nature's orchestra fill the jungle with an ever-growing volume of melody.

And not only the birds, but the animals also, are on the move. A small herd of *cheetal* has crossed the road in front of us, and two hundred yards farther on a *sambhar* hind and her young one are cropping the short grass by the side of the road. A tiger now calls to the east and all the peafowl within hearing distance scream in unison. Kunwar Singh is of opinion that the tiger is the flight of four bullets from us, and that it is in the sandy *nullah* in which he and Har Singh met with their experience which so nearly had a fatal ending. The tiger quite evidently is returning home from a kill and is indifferent as to who sees him. First a *kakar*, then two *sambhar*, and now a herd of *cheetal*, are warning the jungle folk of his presence. We reach Garuppu as the sun is touching the treetops, and crossing the wooden bridge and disturbing fifty or more jungle-fowl that are feeding on the open ground near the ruined staging buildings we take a footpath which leads us through a narrow belt of scrub jungle to the bed of the dry watercourse spanned by the bridge we have just crossed. This watercourse, which is dry except in the heavy monsoon rains, is a highway for all the animals that quench their thirst at the crystal clear spring which rises in its bed three miles farther down. In later years the watercourse became one of my favourite hunting grounds for rifle and camera, for it ran through country which abounded with game, and a human track on its sandy bed was as much a matter for speculation as Friday's footprint on Crusoe's island.

For half a mile the watercourse runs through scrub jungle before entering a strip of *nal* grass a quarter of a mile wide and many miles long. *Nal* grass is hollow, jointed like bamboo, grows to a height of fourteen feet, and when accessible to villages is extensively used for hut building. When the jungles round Garuppu are burnt by our villagers, to get grazing for their cattle, all the game in the vicinity take shelter in the *nal* grass which, because it grows on damp ground, remains green all the year round. During exceptionally dry years, however, the *nal* grass occasionally catches fire, and when this happens a terrifying conflagration results, for the grass is matted together with creepers and each joint of the *nal*, as it heats up bursts with a report resembling a pistol shot, and when millions of joints are exploding at the same time the resulting noise is deafening and can be heard for a mile or more.

As Kunwar Singh and I walked down the watercourse that morning I could see a black cloud of smoke rising high into the sky, and presently the distant roar and crackle of a great fire came to my ears. The watercourse here ran due south and the fire, which was on the eastern or left bank, was being driven towards it by a strong wind. Kunwar Singh was leading and, remarking over his shoulder that the *nal* was burning for the first time in ten years, he kept straight on, and on turning a corner we came in sight of the fire, which was about a hundred yards from the watercourse. Great sheets of flame were curling up into the cloud of black smoke on the edge of which hundreds of starlings, minas, rollers, and drongos were feeding on the winged insects that were being caught up by the hot current of air and whirled high into the sky. Many of the insects that escaped capture by the birds in the air were landing on the sandy bed of the watercourse where they were being pounced on by peafowl, jungle-fowl, and black partridge. Among these game-birds a herd of some twenty *cheetal* were picking up the big red fleshy flowers the high wind was dislodging from a giant *samal* tree.

This was the first forest fire I had ever seen, and I attribute the fear it engendered in me to the fact that most human beings are frightened of the unknown. And then, on rounding the corner and coming in sight of the birds and the animals that were unconcernedly feeding in the vicinity of the fire, I realized that I alone was terrified and that there was no reason, other than ignorance, for my being so. Coming down the watercourse in the wake of Kunwar Singh I had been tempted to turn and run away, and had only been restrained from doing so by the fear of being thought a coward by Kunwar Singh. Now, standing on the sandy bed of the fifty-yard-wide watercourse with the roar of the approaching fire growing louder and louder while black clouds of smoke billowed overhead—waiting for a shootable animal to be driven out of the narrowing belt of *nal* grass—my terror left me, never to return. The heat from the fire could now be felt in the watercourse, and as the deer, peafowl, jungle-fowl, and black partridge climbed the right bank and disappeared into the jungle, we turned and retraced our steps to Garuppu and made for home.

In later years grass-fires provided me with many exciting experiences. Before relating one of these it is necessary for me to state that we who cultivate land at the foot of the Himalayas are permitted, by Government, to burn the grass in unprotected forests to get grazing for our cattle. There are several varieties of grass in these forests and as they do not all dry off at the same time the burning is staggered and, starting in February, ends in June. Throughout this period fires can be seen on the grasslands and anyone passing a patch of grass that he considers is dry enough to burn, is at liberty to put a match to it.

I had been shooting black partridge with Wyndham at Bindukhera in the Tarai, and early one morning Bahadur—an old friend who for thirty years has been headman of our village— and I set out on our twenty-five-mile walk to our home at Kaladhungi. We had covered about ten miles over ground on which most of the grass had been burnt but where there were still a few isolated patches of unburnt grass when, as we approached one of these patches, an animal came out on the cart track we were on, and for a long minute stood broadside on to us. The morning sun was shining on it and from its colouring and size we took it to be a tiger. When, however, it crossed the cart track and entered the grass we saw from the length of its tail that it was a leopard. 'Sahib,' said Bahadur regretfully, 'it is a pity that the Commissioner Sahib and his elephants are ten miles away, for that is the biggest leopard in the Tarai, and it is worth shooting.' That the leopard was worth shooting there was no question, and even though Wyndham and his elephants were ten miles away, I decided to have a try, for the leopard had come from the direction of a cattle station, and the fact that he was moving about in the open at that hour of the day was proof that he was coming from a kill he had made overnight at this station. When I outlined my plan—to burn the leopard out—to Bahadur, he expressed his willingness to help, but was doubtful of its success. The first thing to do was to find out how big the patch of grass was, so leaving the cart track we circled round it and found it was some ten acres in extent and cone shaped, with the cart track running along the base.

The wind was right for my plan, so going to the farthest point of the grass, which was about two hundred yards from the cart track, I cut two tufts of grass and lighting them sent Bahadur to set fire to the grass on the right, while I set fire to it on the left. It was of the variety known as elephant grass, some twelve feet in height, and as dry as tinder, and within a minute of our setting it alight it was burning fiercely. Running back to the cart track I lay down on it and putting my rifle, a ·275 Rigby, to my shoulder I took a sight along the outer edge of the track at a height that would put my bullet in the leopard's body when he tried to dash across it. I was lying ten yards from the grass, and the point where the leopard had entered it was fifty yards from me. The track was ten feet wide and my only hope of hitting the leopard was to press the trigger the moment I caught sight of him, for I was convinced he would cross the track at the last moment, and cross it at speed. There was no possibility of injury to Bahadur for I had instructed him to climb a tree, well clear of the track, after he had set a short stretch of the grass on fire.

Half the grass had been burnt and the roar from the fire was like an express train going over a trestle bridge, when I saw a bare human foot near my right shoulder. On looking up I found a man standing near me who, from his appearance and dress, I knew was a Mahommedan cartman probably out looking for a lost bullock. Reaching up I pulled the man down and yelled into his ear to lie still beside me, and to ensure his doing so I threw a leg across him. On came the fire and when only some twenty-five yards of grass remained to be burnt the leopard streaked across the track and as I pressed the trigger I saw its tail go up. The grass on the left-hand side of the track had been burnt some days previously, and the forest of burnt stalks into which the leopard had disappeared made it impossible for me to see what the result of my shot had been. Reassured, however, by the way the leopard's tail had gone up that he was fatally wounded, I sprang up, took a firm grip of the man's hand, jerked him to his feet, and ran with him down the cart track through a dense cloud of smoke with the flames of the oncoming fire curling dangerously over our heads. Not until we were right over him did we see the leopard, and without losing a moment—for the heat here was terrific—I stooped down and putting the man's hand on the leopard's tail closed my hand over his and as we pulled the leopard round to drag it away from the fire the animal, to my horror, opened its mouth and snarled at us. Fortunately for us my bullet had gone through its neck and paralysed it, and by the time we had dragged it fifty yards to safety it was dead. As I released my hold on the man's hand he sprang away from me as though I had bitten him, and grabbing the *pugree* off his head ran with it trailing behind him as no cartman had ever run before.

I regret I was not present when my friend arrived at whatever destination he was making for. Indians are past masters at recounting tales, and my friend's tale of his escape from the clutches of a mad Englishman would have been worth listening to. Bahadur had witnessed the whole occurrence from his perch on the tree and when he rejoined me he said, 'That man will be very popular at camp-fires for many years to come, but no one will believe his story.'

When conditions are not favourable for walking up so-called dangerous animals and shooting them on foot, the method most generally employed is to beat them out of cover with the help of elephants or men, or a combination of the two. Three of these beats stand out in my memory as being worthy of record, if for no other reason than that two were carried out with the minimum of manpower, while the third provided me with an experience that makes my heart miss a beat or two every time I think of it.

First Beat

Robin—our springer spaniel—and I were out for a walk one morning on the fire track half a mile to the west of the Boar bridge. Robin was leading, and on coming to a spot where there was short grass on the little-used track he stopped, smelt the grass, and then turned his head and looked at me. On going up to him I could see no tracks, so I signalled to him to follow the scent he had found. Very deliberately he turned to the left and, on reaching the edge of the track, ran his nose up and down a blade of grass and then with a quick glance round at me, as if to say, 'It's all right, I was not mistaken', stepped into the grass which here was about eighteen inches high. Foot by foot he followed the scent and a hundred yards farther on, where there was a little depression with damp earth in it, I saw he was trailing a tiger. On the far side of the depression Robin intently examined a blade of grass, and on stooping down I saw he had found a spot of blood. From experiences I have had with animals left wounded in the jungles by others I am very suspicious of any blood I find on a tiger track. However, on this occasion it was all right for the blood was quite fresh, and no shots had been fired in this direction that morning, so I concluded the tiger was carrying a kill, possibly a *cheetal*, or maybe a big pig. A few yards farther on there was a dense patch of clerodendron some fifty yards square, on reaching which Robin stopped and looked round at me for further instructions.

I recognized the tiger from his pug marks on the damp earth.

He was a big tiger who had taken up his residence in the heavy scrub jungle on the far side of the Boar river and who, since our descent from the hills three months previously, had given me a lot of anxiety. The two roads and the fire track on which Maggie and I were accustomed to take our morning and evening walks ran through this jungle, and on several occasions when I was away from home Maggie and Robin had encountered the tiger while out for a walk. On each succeeding occasion the tiger had shown less inclination to give way to them and the stage had been reached when Robin no longer considered it was safe for Maggie to walk on these roads, and flatly refused to accompany her beyond the bridge. Fearing that some day there might be an accident I had decided to take the first opportunity that offered to shoot the tiger, and now—provided the tiger was lying up with his kill in the patch of clerodendron—the opportunity I had been waiting for had come. Robin had trailed the tiger down wind, so making a wide detour I approached the clerodendron from the opposite side. When we were thirty yards away Robin halted, raised his head into the wind, jerked his muzzle up and down a few times, and then looked round at me. Good enough. The tiger was there all right, so we regained the fire track and made for home.

After breakfast I sent for Bahadur, told him about the tiger, and asked him to fetch two of our tenants, Dhanban and Dharmanand, both of whom could be relied on to carry out instructions, and both of whom were as expert at tree climbing as Bahadur and myself. By midday the three men had eaten their food and forgathered at our cottage, and after seeing that they had nothing in their pockets that would rattle I made them remove their shoes and arming myself with a 450/400 rifle, we set off. On the way I outlined my plans for the beat I intended the three men to carry out. The men knew the jungle as well as I did and when I told them where the tiger was lying up, and what I wanted them to do, they were full of enthusiasm. My

plan was to put the men up on trees on three sides of the patch
of clerodendron, to stir the tiger up while I guarded the fourth
side. Bahadur was to be on the central tree and on receiving a
signal from me, which would be the call of a leopard, he was
to tap a branch and if the tiger tried to break out on either
side the man nearest to it was to clap his hands. The essence
of the whole enterprise was silence, for the three men would
be within thirty or forty yards of the tiger and the slightest sound
while approaching their trees, climbing them, or while waiting
for my signal, would ruin the plan.

On reaching the spot where Robin had picked up the tiger's
scent I made Dhanban and Dharmanand sit down, while I took
Bahadur and put him up a tree twenty yards from the
clerodendron, and opposite where I intended taking my stand.
Then one by one I took the other two men and put them up
in trees to Bahadur's right and left. All three men were in sight
of each other, and all three overlooked the patch of clerodendron
and would, therefore, be able to see any movement the tiger
made, but they would be screened from me by a belt of trees.
After the last man was safely on his tree, without a sound having
been made, I went back to the fire track and going a hundred
yards up it met—at right angles—another fire track that skirted
the foot of a long low hill. This second fire track bordered the
patch of clerodendron on its fourth side. Opposite the tree on
which Bahadur was sitting, a narrow and shallow ravine ran up
the side of the hill. The ravine was much used by game and I
felt sure the tiger on being disturbed would make for it. On
the right-hand side of the ravine, and ten yards up the hill,
there was a big *jamun* tree. When planning the beat I had
intended sitting on this tree and shooting the tiger as he went
up the ravine past me. But now, on reaching the tree, I found
I could not climb it with the heavy rifle in my hands and as
there were no other trees nearby I decided to sit on the ground.

So, clearing the dry leaves from the root, I sat down with my back to the tree.

I had two reasons for giving the call of a leopard. One, a signal to Bahadur to start tapping a branch with the dry stick I had left with him: the other, to reassure the tiger that it was safe for him to cross the fire track, and to disarm any suspicion he may have had that he was being driven towards danger. When I was comfortably seated on the ground I pushed up the safety catch and putting the rifle to my shoulder, gave the call of a leopard. A few seconds later Bahadur started tapping with his stick and he had only tapped a few times when the bushes parted and a magnificent tiger stepped out on the fire track and came to a stand. For ten years I had been trying to get a cine-photograph of a tiger, and though I had seen tigers on many occasions I had not succeeded in getting one satisfactory picture. And now out in the open, twenty yards from me with not a leaf nor a blade of grass between us, and the sun shining on his beautifully marked winter coat, was a tiger that I would have gone anywhere and given anything to photograph. I have on occasions stalked an animal, maybe for hours or maybe for days, and on getting up to it raised my rifle and after taking careful aim lowered it, and then attracting the animal's attention flourished my hat, giving myself the pleasure of seeing it bound away unhurt. I would very gladly have treated this tiger in the same way, but I did not feel that I would be justified in doing so. Apart from consideration of Maggie, Sher Singh and other small boys grazed their cattle in this jungle, and the women and children of the village collected dry sticks in it, and though the tiger had not harmed man or beast his method of demonstrating was very terrifying and might easily result in an accident.

After stepping out on the fire track the tiger stood for a minute or two looking to his right and to his left, and over his

shoulder in the direction of Bahadur. Then very leisurely he crossed the track and started up the hill on the left-hand side of the ravine. My sights had been on him from the time his head parted the clerodendron bushes, and when he was level with me I pressed the trigger. I do not think he so much as heard my shot, and as his legs folded up under him he slid backwards and came to rest near my feet.

Beat No. 2

When His Highness the Maharaja of Jind died—full of years and loved by all who knew him—India lost one of her finest sportsmen. Ruler of a territory of 1,299 square miles with a population of 324,700 and a princely rent-roll, the Maharaja was one of the most unassuming men it has been my good fortune to meet. His hobbies were training gun-dogs and tiger shooting, and at both these sports he had few equals. When I first knew him he had four hundred dogs in his kennels and to see him schooling young dogs, and later handling them in the field, was a lesson in patience and gentleness that I never tired of watching. Only once did I ever hear the Maharaja raise his voice, or use a whip, to a dog. At dinner that night when the Maharani asked if the dogs had behaved themselves the Maharaja said, 'No, Sandy was very disobedient and I had to give him a good thrashing.'

The Maharaja and I had been out bird shooting that day. A long strip of grass and bush jungle was being beaten towards us by a line of elephants and men. At the end of the strip was an open stretch of ground some fifty yards wide. The Maharaja and I were standing a few yards apart at the farther edge of the open ground, with short grass behind us. Sitting in a row to the Maharaja's left were three young Labradors, Sandy golden coloured, the other two black. The line put up a black partridge and the Maharaja dropped it on the open ground and sent one of the black dogs to retrieve it. Next a jungle-fowl came low over my head and I dropped it in the grass behind me. The second black dog retrieved this bird. Some peafowl now got up, but having heard the shots in front, broke away to the left and passed out of range. A hare then broke cover and checking at the Maharaja, who had turned round to speak to a servant behind him, turned at right angles and passed in front of me. Waiting until it was at extreme range—for it is not advisable to break game more than can be helped when young dogs are in the field—I fired, and the hare turned about and passing in front of both of us collapsed thirty yards to the right of the Maharaja. As it went over Sandy shot forward. 'Sandy, *Sandy*,' shouted the Maharaja, but Sandy was listening to no one. His two companions had retrieved their birds and it was his turn now and nothing was going to stop him. In his stride he picked up the hare and racing back handed it to me. Returning to his

master Sandy sat down in his allotted place, and was ordered
to fetch the hare. Picking it up from where I had laid it down
he trotted towards the Maharaja with it held high, and was
waved away, farther, farther, to the right, still farther, until he
reached the spot from where he had originally retrieved it. Here
he was told to drop it and signalled to return. With drooping
tail and hanging ears Sandy returned to his master a second
time, and one of the other dogs was sent out to bring in the
hare. When this had been done the Maharaja handed his gun
to his servant, and taking a whip from him, caught Sandy by
the scruff of his neck and gave him 'a good thrashing'. And a
good thrashing it was but not for Sandy, for he was not touched,
but for the ground on either side of him. When the Maharaja
told his wife of Sandy's delinquency and the chastisement he
had administered, I took a tablet from an attendant behind
me—for the Maharaja was afflicted with total deafness—and
wrote on it, 'Though Sandy Bahadur disobeyed you today he is
the best dog in India, and will win the championship at the
next gun-dog trials.' Later that year I received a telegram from
the Maharaja which read, 'You were quite right. Sandy has won
the Open Championship.'

The days were lengthening and the sun was getting hot, so
making a very early start one morning I walked ten miles and
arrived at the Maharaja's camp at Mohan as the family were
sitting down to breakfast. 'You have come at a very opportune
time,' said the Maharaja as I took a seat at his table, 'for today
we are going to beat for the old tiger that has eluded us for
three years.' I had heard this tiger discussed on many occasions
and knew how keen the Maharaja was to outwit and shoot it.
When, therefore, he offered me the best of the three *machans*
that had been put up for the beat, and the loan of a rifle, I
declined his offer and said I would prefer to be a spectator. At

ten o'clock the Maharaja and Maharani, their two daughters and
a girl friend and I motored down the road up which I had walked
earlier that morning, to where the beat was waiting for us.

The ground to be beaten was a valley running deep into the
foothills, with a small stream winding through it, and flanked
on either side by hills three hundred feet high. At its lower
end, where the road crossed it, the valley
was about fifty yards wide, and half a
mile farther up it again narrowed to fifty
yards. Between these two points the
valley widened out to three or four
hundred yards and here, where there was a
dense patch of cover several hundred acres in
extent, the tiger was thought to be lying
up with the buffalo he had killed
the previous night. At the upper
end of the valley a small spur
ran down from the hill on the
right, and on a tree on this spur,
a *machan* had been built which
commanded the valley and the
lower slopes of the hills on either
side. Beyond the spur and on the far
side of the stream, which here turned at right angles, two other
machans had been put up on trees thirty yards apart.

Leaving our cars on the road we proceeded up the valley on
foot, and guided by the head *shikari* and the secretary in charge
of the beat, skirted to the left of the cover in which the tiger
was said to be lying. When the Maharaja and his gun-bearer
had taken their seats on the *machan* on the spur, the four ladies
and I crossed the stream and occupied the two *machans* on the

far side of it. The head *shikari* and the secretary then left us, and returned to the road to start the beat.

The *machan* I was on, with the two princesses, was a solidly-built affair laid with a thick carpet, with silk cushions to sit on. Accustomed only to sitting on hard branches, the luxury of the *machan*—following on an early rise and a long walk—made me drowsy and I was on the point of falling asleep when I was roused to full wakefulness by the distant sound of a bugle; the beat had started. Taking part in the beat were ten elephants, the Secretaries, A.D.C.s, household staff of the Maharaja, the head *shikari* and his assistants, and two hundred men collected from the surrounding villages. The heavy cover on the floor of the valley was to be beaten by the elephants on which the Secretaries and others were mounted, while the two hundred men beat the slopes on either side. Some of these beaters were to form a line on the two ridges and walk ahead of the beat to prevent the tiger from breaking out.

All the arrangements for the beat, and the beat itself, were intensely interesting for me for I was witnessing as a spectator an event in which I had hitherto always been an actor. There was nothing in the arrangements or in the conduct of the beat that could be found fault with. The time of day had been well chosen; we had been led to our *machans* in perfect silence; and that the cover was being well beaten was evident from the number of birds, including *kalege* pheasants, jungle-fowl, and peafowl, that the line was putting up. Beats are always exciting, for from the moment the distant shouting of the men is heard, the tiger can be expected to be on the move. The Maharaja was handicapped by deafness but he had a good man with him, and presently I saw this man pointing to the right. After looking in this direction for a moment or two the Maharaja shook his head, and a little later a *sambhar* stag crossed the stream and on winding the Maharaja dashed past us up the valley.

The line of men on the ridge on the left was now visible, and the time had come for the tiger to appear. On came the beat with every man taking part in it shouting and clapping his hands, and every yard they advanced my hopes of the Maharaja shooting the tiger on which he had set his heart diminished, for no bird or animal had given an alarm-call. My young companions on the *machan* were keyed up, and the Maharaja was holding his rifle ready, for if the tiger appeared now he would have to take a quick shot. But rifles were of no use today, for the tiger was not in the beat. Ladders were produced and a very dejected party climbed down from the *machans* and joined an even more dejected staff on the ground. No one engaged in the beat had seen anything of the tiger, and no one knew what had gone wrong. But that something had gone wrong was evident, for shortly before our arrival in the cars the tiger had been heard calling in the valley. I had a suspicion

that I knew why the beat had miscarried but, as I was only a spectator, I said nothing. After a picnic lunch we returned to camp, and while the others rested I went off and had a grand evening's fishing on the Kosi, for it was the latter end of April and the fishing was at its best.

During and after dinner that night, the abortive beat of the day and five previous unsuccessful beats for the same tiger were discussed in minute detail and a reason sought for their failure. On the first occasion on which a beat had been organized in the valley for this particular tiger, he had come out on the right of the machan and the Maharaja, taking an awkward shot from a fixed seat, had missed him. In the succeeding beats, carried out over a period of three years, the tiger had not again been seen, though he was known to have been in the valley before the beats started. While the others had been talking and writing on tablets for the Maharaja's benefit, I had been thinking. The Maharaja was a good sportsman, and if I could help him to shoot the tiger on which he had set his heart it was up to me to try. A mistake had been made that day in taking the Maharaja's party to the machans, past the spot where the tiger was thought to be lying up, but this mistake was not responsible for the failure of the beat, for the tiger had left the valley at about the time the Maharaja's party had entered it. The single alarm-call of a kakar, heard shortly after we had left our cars, was all the foundation I had for my suspicion that the tiger walked out of the valley as we walked into it. Later when it became evident that an empty jungle had been beaten, I looked round to see if there was any other way for the tiger to leave the valley without passing the machans. Starting on the ridge behind the machans a landslide extended right down into the valley. The kakar had called at the upper end of this landslide and if there was a game track here running down to the cover in which the tiger had his kill, then it was quite possible that he left the valley by this track every time he heard preparations being made for a beat.

The plan that had been forming in my mind while the others talked was to put the Maharaja on the ridge, where the *kakar* had called, and beat the tiger up to him. Beating a second time for the tiger on the following day had been vetoed by every one, on the ground that as the tiger had not been found on a fresh kill there was no hope of finding him on a stale one. So even if my plan failed no harm would be done, for no arrangements had been made for the following day. Taking a tablet from one of the secretaries I wrote on it, 'If you can be ready at 5 a.m. tomorrow, I should like to do a one-man beat for the tiger we failed to get today', and handed the paper to the Maharaja. After reading what I had written the Maharaja passed the paper to his secretary, and from hand to hand it went round the room. I expected opposition from the staff, and it came now. However, as the Maharaja was willing to fall in with my plans, the staff reluctantly agreed to all conventions being set aside, and to the Maharaja going out with me next morning accompanied only by two gun-bearers.

Punctually at 5 a.m. the Maharaja, his two gun-bearers, and I, left the camp by car and motored three miles down the road to where an elephant, carrying a small *machan*, was waiting for us. Transferring the Maharaja and his two men to the elephant I set out on foot to guide the elephant through several miles of forest in which I had never been before. Fortunately I have a sense of direction, and though it was dark when we started I was able to steer a more or less straight course, and as the sun was rising we arrived on the ridge where the landslide started. Here I was delighted to find a well-used game-track leading up from the valley, and on a tree near the track I put up the *machan*. When the Maharaja and one gun-bearer had taken their seats on the *machan* I sent the elephant away, and taking the other gun-bearer with me, put him up on a tree farther along the ridge. These preparations completed, I set off to do a one-man beat.

The way down into the valley was terribly steep and rough, but as I was not hampered with a rifle, I accomplished the descent safely. Passing the machans we had sat on the previous day, I went down the valley on silent feet, and two hundred yards beyond the heavy cover in which I suspected the tiger was lying, I turned and retraced my steps, talking to myself in a low voice as I did so. Where the tiger dragged the buffalo into the heavy cover there was a fallen tree. Lighting a cigarette I sat down on this tree, to listen if the jungle had anything to tell me. All remained quiet, so after coughing a few times and drumming my heels against the hollow tree I set out to find the kill and see if the tiger had returned to it. I found the kill tucked away under some thick bushes and was delighted to see that the tiger had eaten a meal only a few minutes previously, and that the ground on which he had been lying was still warm. Running back to the hollow tree I hammered on it with a stone and shouted at the top of my voice, to let the man with the Maharaja know that the tiger was coming. A minute or two later a rifle shot rang out above me, and when I got to the ridge I found the Maharaja standing on the game track, looking at the fine tiger he had shot.

In the palace at Jind, now occupied by the Maharaja's eldest son, there is a skin with a label which reads, 'Jim's Tiger'. And in the late Maharaja's game-book there is an entry giving the date and place, and the circumstances in which the old tiger was shot.

Beat No. 3

It was the last day of a memorable shoot. Memorable not only for us who had been privileged to take part in it, but also for the administrators of the country, for a Viceroy had for the first time in the history of India left the beaten track to spend a few days in the Kaladhungi jungles.

No individual's movements were more strictly ruled by precedents than the movements of the Viceroy of India, and any deviation from the beaten track was a contingency that had never been contemplated, and for which no provision had been made. When, therefore, Lord Linlithgow, shortly after assuming the Viceroyalty of India, decided to leave the track his predecessors had followed and blaze a track for himself, it was only natural that his decision should have caused consternation throughout the land. Custom decreed that the ruler of India should tour the southern provinces of his domain during the ten days hiatus between the closing of his Legislative Offices in Delhi and their reopening in Simla, and it was Lord Linlithgow's decision not to conform with this age-old custom that caused the long to be remembered flutter in the government dovecotes.

I, a mere man in the street without any connexion with Government, was happily ignorant of the working of wheels within wheels of the administration when one day, towards the end of March, as I was setting out from our cottage at Kaladhungi to catch a fish for our dinner, Ram Singh, whose duty it was to fetch our daily post from the Post Office two miles away, came running back with a telegram which he said the Postmaster had informed him was very urgent. The telegram, which had been redirected from Naini Tal, was from Hugh Stable, Military Secretary to the Viceroy. It informed me that the Viceroy's visit to South India had been cancelled, and asked if I could suggest any place where the Viceroy could spend ten days, with the possibility of getting a little shooting before proceeding to Simla for the summer. The telegram concluded with a request for an early reply, as time was short, and the matter urgent. Ram Singh does not speak English but having served us for thirty years he can understand it, and having stood round finding odd jobs to do while I read the telegram to Maggie, he now said he would hurry up and have his food and be ready in a few minutes to take my reply to Haldwani. Haldwani—our nearest telegraph and telephone office—is fourteen miles from Kaladhungi and by sending my reply by Ram Singh, instead of by the regular dak runner, I would save a matter of some twenty-four hours. After Ram Singh had left with my reply to Hugh Stable which read, 'Please call me on Haldwani telephone at eleven hours tomorrow', I picked up my rod for the second time, for one can do a lot of thinking while fishing and I had much to think about, and, further, I still had our dinner to catch. Hugh Stable's telegram was quite clearly in the nature of an SOS, and the question I had to decide was, what could I do help him?

Going up the Kota road for two miles I cut across the lower end of the Farm Yard—where when a small boy I shot my first leopard—and made for a pool in the river in which a three-pound *mahseer* with whom I was acquainted lived. As I approached the pool I saw in the sand the pug marks of a tiger that had crossed the river early that morning. At the head of the pool, where the water runs fast and deep, there are three big rocks a foot above water which are continually wet with spray and in consequence as slippery as ice. Leopards use these rocks as stepping stones and one day I saw the tiger, whose pug marks were now on the sand, trying to do the same. I had chased the tiger that day for a mile without his knowing I was after him and twice I got to within shooting range, and on both occasions held my fire as I was not sure of killing him outright. And then as I saw he was making for the river I just kept him in sight for I knew I would get the shot I wanted when he was fording the river. As he approached the river it became evident that he intended crossing it dryshod by way of the stepping stones, and not wading it as I at first thought he intended doing. This suited me admirably for there was a twenty-foot drop on our side down which the tiger would have to go before reaching the river, and as he went over the edge to climb down I ran forward and lay down on the top of the bank above him.

The three rocks were at a distance apart that an Olympian athlete could, if he had a good run, have taken in a hop, skip, and jump, and which I had seen leopards do in three graceful bounds. The tiger had just accomplished the first jump safely as I poked my head over the edge, but he bungled the second jump, and as his feet shot off the slippery rock he went heels over head into the deep and broken water. The noise from the water prevented my hearing what he said, but I could guess what it was for I had myself slipped on that self-same rock while trying to cross the river dryshod. On the far side of the broken water there is a short beach of dry sand. Floundering out on to this beach the tiger shook himself and then lay down and rolled over and over, drying his beautiful rich winter coat in the hot sand. Then getting to his feet he shook himself for a second time and walked quietly away to whatever place he was making for, without let or hindrance from me, for in the jungle it is not considered cricket to molest an animal that has provided entertainment. And now the pug marks of the tiger were showing on the sand again, but this time he had essayed the stepping stones safely for his feet when he crossed the sand had been dry.

Below the stepping stones a rock jutted out from the far bank making a backwater which was my friend the three-pounder's favourite hunting ground. Twice before a Jock Scott cast on the sloping rock and gently drawn off, had brought the *mahseer* out with a rush. The throw was a long and a difficult one, for the branch of a tree hung low over the backwater and the rod had to be used from a crouching position, for *mahseer* who have enemies on land, in the air, and in the water, are keen of sight and need a careful approach. Leaving the sandy beach, with the pug marks on it, I went upstream for a short distance, and while the ten-foot tapered cast I made that morning from carefully selected lengths of gut was soaking under a stone, put my rod together and had a smoke. When all was ready I pulled what I considered to be the exact length of line off the reel, and holding it carefully looped in my left hand crept down to the one spot from where it was possible to make a sideways cast on to the rock, for the bank behind did not permit of an orthodox cast. The new No. 8 Jock Scott put on in honour of the three-pounder landed exactly where I wanted it to, and as the drag of the line drew it off the rock into deep water, there was a swirl and a splash and for the third time my friend was well and truly hooked. It is not possible, when using light tackle, to stop the first mad rush of a *mahseer*, but by using just the right amount of strain he can be guided away from any snag he is making for, provided the snag is not on the same side of the river as the angler. I was fishing from the right bank and thirty yards below where I had hooked the fish a curved root jutted out into the water. On the two previous occasions the fish had broken me on this root, but I managed to steer him clear of it now with only a few inches to spare. Once he was in the pool, he was safe, and after letting him play himself out I drew him to the sandy beach and landed him by hand, for I had brought no landing net with me. My estimate of three pounds was half a pound out, on the right side, so not only would he furnish us with a dinner, but he would also provide a meal for a sick boy Maggie was nursing in the village, who loved fish above all other things.

Having followed the advice given me on the rifle range when I was a boy, by sending Hugh Stable a non-committal telegram, I had given myself ample time to think, and to what extent my seeing the pug marks of the tiger and my success with the *mahseer* influenced my decision I cannot say; anyway, by the time I got home I had decided to tell Hugh Stable that Kaladhungi was the only place I could suggest for the Viceroy's holiday. Maggie had tea ready on the veranda and while we were talking over the decision I had come to, Bahadur arrived. Bahadur can keep

his mouth shut when there is any necessity to do so, so I told
him about the telegram I had received from Delhi. Bahadur's
eyes literally dance when he is excited, and I have never seen
them dance as they did that day. A possibility of the Viceroy
coming to Kaladhungi! Why, such a thing had never before been
heard of. A great *bandobast* would have to be made and
fortunately it was just the right time of the year to make it, for
the crops had been harvested and every man in the village would
be available. Later, when it became known that the Viceroy was
coming to our jungles, not only our own tenants but every
man in Kaladhungi was as excited and as pleased as Bahadur
had been when he heard the news. Not because of any profit
or preferment they hoped to derive from the visit, but simply
and solely because of their desire to help in their own humble
way to make the visit a success.

It was dark when I started on my fourteen-mile walk to
Haldwani next morning, for I wanted to see Geoff Hopkins,
who was camped at Fatehpur, before my conversation with Hugh
Stable. The road runs through jungle for the first seven miles
and at that hour of the morning the jungle folk and I had it to
ourselves. A mile beyond the Kaladhungi bazaar it started to
get light and in the dust of the road I saw the fresh pug marks
of a male leopard, going in the same direction as I was. Presently,
on rounding a bend in the road, I saw the leopard two hundred
yards ahead of me. He seemed to sense my presence for I had
hardly rounded the bend when he turned his head and looked
at me. However, he kept to the road, occasionally looking over
his shoulder, and when I had reduced the distance between us
to fifty yards, he stepped off the road into a light patch of grass.
Keeping steadily on and looking straight ahead, out of the corner
of my eye I saw him crouched down in the grass a few feet from
the road. A hundred yards along when I looked over my shoulder

I saw he was back on the road. To him I was just a wayfarer for whom he had made way, and a few hundred yards farther on he left the road and entered a deep ravine. For a mile I had the road to myself, and then out of the jungle on the right trotted five red dogs. Fleet of foot, and fearless; flitting through the forests as silent and free as a butterfly, and when hungry, eating only of the best. Of all the animals I know none has a better life, than the Indian red dog.

Geoff and Zillah Hopkins were sitting down to an early breakfast when I reached the forest bungalow, and were as pleased and excited as they could be when I told them of the errand on which I was going to Haldwani. Geoff was at that time Special Forest Officer, Tarai and Bhabar Government Estates, and without his help and co-operation I could make no concrete suggestions to Hugh Stable. Geoff rose nobly to the occasion. For the success of the shoot it was essential for me to have two shooting blocks in his forests. Both the blocks I wanted were fortunately available at the time, and Geoff said he would reserve them for me. He also very kindly offered me the Dachauri block in the adjoining government forest, which he had reserved for himself. Everything, from seeing the pug marks of the tiger in the sand, the catching of the *mahseer*, and now my successful visit to Geoff, was going splendidly, and I never felt the miles as they passed under my feet as I completed my journey to Haldwani.

Hugh Stable was on the telephone punctually at eleven o'clock and for the next hour we carried on an uninterrupted conversation, over the three-hundred-mile-long line. In that hour Hugh learnt that there was a small village at the foothills of the Himalayas called Kaladhungi; that this village was surrounded by jungles in which there was a variety of game; and that I knew of no place in India where a more pleasant holiday could be spent. From Hugh I learnt that the Viceregal party would consist of Their Excellencies Lord and Lady Linlithgow, and their three daughters, the Ladies Anne, Joan, and Doreen (Bunty) Hope. With the party would come H.E.'s personal staff, for even when on holiday the Viceroy of India does a full day's work. Finally I learnt I had only fifteen days in which to make all my preparations for the shoot. Mouse Maxwell, the Controller of the Viceroy's Household, motored from Delhi to Kaladhungi the following day, and he was followed by the head of the Police, the head of the C.I.D., the head of the Civil Administration, the head of the Forest Department, and by many other heads. But most terrifying of all by a Guardsman who informed me he was bringing a company of soldiers to Kaladhungi to guard the person of the Viceroy.

Bahadur had been right when he said a great *bandobast* would have to be made, but how great that *bandobast* would have to be neither he nor I had dreamed. However, with the whole-hearted help and co-operation of all concerned everything had progressed smoothly and well, without a single hitch or set-back. Four beats had been successfully carried out and four tigers had been cleanly shot, with the minimum expenditure of ammunition, by people who had never before seen tigers in the wilds. Only those who have taken part in tiger beats will know how great an achievement this had been. And now the last day of that memorable shoot had come with only one, the youngest, member of the party left to shoot a tiger. The beat that day was to take place on a semi-circular bit of ground which in bygone years had been the bed of the Boar river, but which now is clothed with dense tree and scrub jungle interspersed with small patches of *nal* grass, and thickets of wild oranges. Five *machans* had been built in trees on what

at one time had been the bank of the river, and the tiger was
to be beaten off the low ground towards these *machans*.

Making a wide detour, for many beats are ruined by taking
the guns to their *machans* past the cover in which the tiger is
assumed to be lying up, I brought the party up from behind
the *machans* and while the stops, who had accompanied us,
fanned out to right and left to take up position on the trees I
had previously marked for them, Peter Borwick (one of H.E.'s
A.D.C.s), Bahadur, and I, started to put the guns in position.
On No. 1 *machan* I put Anne, and on No. 2 *machan* I put H.E.
No. 3 *machan* had been built in the only tree available at this
spot, a stunted *kart bair* (wood plum) tree. It had been my
intention to put Bahadur on this *machan* to act as a stop. On
being stopped I expected the tiger to turn to the left, and for
this reason I had selected No. 4 *machan* for Bunty, the only
member of the party who had not shot a tiger.

Coming from the direction of the cover, in which I knew
the tiger was lying up, a game-track ran up the bank and passed
right under No. 3 *machan*. I was certain the tiger would come
along this track and as the *machan* was only six feet above ground
I had decided that, though it would be quite safe to put an
experienced stop on it, it would be too dangerous for a gun.
Now, however, as the two girls, Peter, Bahadur, and I, reached
the *machan* and Bahadur started to climb on to it, on the spur
of the moment I changed my plans. Putting my hand on the
machan, which was on a level with my head, I whispered to
Bunty that I wanted her to sit on it with Peter to keep her
company. This—after I had pointed out the danger—she
consented to do without a moment's hesitation. I then begged
her not to shoot at the tiger until it reached a spot on the
track that I would mark, and to take very careful aim at its
throat. Bunty promised to do both of these things, so Peter

and I lifted her on to the *machan*. After I had given Peter a leg
up I handed him my 450/400 D.B. rifle, a similar weapon to
the one Bunty was armed with. (Peter was unarmed, for he
was to have accompanied me in the beat.) Then going down
the bank I walked up the game-track, and when within twenty
feet of the *machan*, laid a dry stick across the track and as I did
so I looked up at Bunty and she nodded her head.

Lady Joan, Bahadur, and I, now went to the tree on which
No. 4 *machan* had been built. This *machan* was twenty feet above
ground and from it to No. 3 *machan*—thirty yards away—there
was a clear and uninterrupted view. When I climbed the ladder
after Joan to hand her rifle, I begged her not to allow the tiger
to reach No. 3 *machan* if Bunty and Peter failed to stop it. 'I
will do my best,' she said, adding, 'don't you worry.' There
were no bushes and only a few scattered trees on this part of
the bank, and the tiger would be in full view of these two
machans from the time it left the cover sixty yards away until it
was, I hoped, shot dead by Bunty. Putting Bahadur on No. 5
machan, to act as a stop if necessary, I circled outside the beat
and came out on to the Boar river.

The sixteen elephants that were to do the beating were
collected a quarter of a mile down the river, near the pool in
which I caught the *mahseer*. They were in charge of old Mohan,
a friend of many years standing, who for thirty years had been
Wyndham's head *shikari*, and who knew more about tigers than
any man in India. Mohan was on the look-out for me, and on
seeing me come out of the jungle and wave my hat he started
the elephants up the bed of the river. Sixteen elephants walking
in line over boulder-strewn ground take some time to cover a
quarter of a mile, and while I sat on a rock and smoked I had
ample time to think, and the more I thought the more uneasy
I became. For the first time in my life I was endangering the

life of one, and quite possibly two, human beings, and the fact that it was the first time gave me little comfort. Before his arrival in Kaladhungi Lord Linlithgow asked me to draw up a set of rules. These rules had been scrupulously obeyed, and with over three hundred people in camp, and daily excursions to near and distant shooting and fishing grounds, no one had received so much as a scratch. And now on this last day I, whom everyone trusted, had done a thing that I was bitterly regretting. On a frail *machan*, only six feet above ground, and on which I would not have trusted any man of my acquaintance, I had put a young girl little more than sixteen years of age to shoot a tiger as it came straight towards her, the most dangerous shot that one can take at a tiger. Both Bunty and Peter were as brave as tigers, as was abundantly evident by the fact that after I had pointed out the danger to them they had unhesitatingly taken their seats on the *machan*. But bravery alone without accuracy of aim would not be sufficient, and of their ability to hold a rifle straight I had no knowledge. Mohan arrived with the elephants while I was still undecided whether to call off the beat or go on with it, and when I told him what I had done he drew in his breath—the Indian equivalent to the Western whistle—closed his eyes tight and on reopening them said, 'Don't *ghabrao* (worry) Sahib. Everything will be all right.'

Calling the mahouts together I told them it was very essential for us to move the tiger without frightening it, and that after lining-out on the river bank they would take their signal from me. When they saw me take my hat off and wave it they would give one shout, after which they would clap their hands and continue to clap them until I replaced the hat on my head. This procedure would be repeated at short intervals and if it failed to move the tiger I would give the

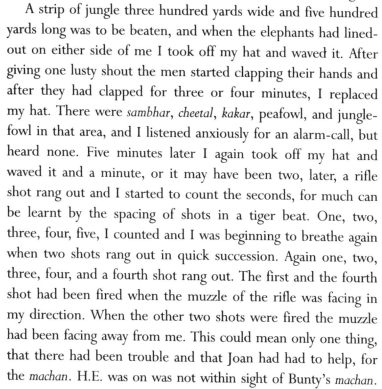

signal to advance, and the advance would be made in silence and dead slow. Our initial shout would serve a double purpose, it would rouse the tiger from his sleep, and it would alert the guns.

A strip of jungle three hundred yards wide and five hundred yards long was to be beaten, and when the elephants had lined-out on either side of me I took off my hat and waved it. After giving one lusty shout the men started clapping their hands and after they had clapped for three or four minutes, I replaced my hat. There were *sambhar*, *cheetal*, *kakar*, peafowl, and jungle-fowl in that area, and I listened anxiously for an alarm-call, but heard none. Five minutes later I again took off my hat and waved it and a minute, or it may have been two, later, a rifle shot rang out and I started to count the seconds, for much can be learnt by the spacing of shots in a tiger beat. One, two, three, four, five, I counted and I was beginning to breathe again when two shots rang out in quick succession. Again one, two, three, four, and a fourth shot rang out. The first and the fourth shot had been fired when the muzzle of the rifle was facing in my direction. When the other two shots were fired the muzzle had been facing away from me. This could mean only one thing, that there had been trouble and that Joan had had to help, for the *machan*. H.E. was on was not within sight of Bunty's *machan*.

With my heart racing and fears assailing me that I was too frightened to give expression to, I handed over the line to Mohan to bring up and told Ajmat, the mahout of the elephant I was on, to go as fast as he could straight to where the shots had been fired. Ajmat, who has been trained by Wyndham, is absolutely fearless and the best man on an elephant I have ever known. And his elephant is as well trained and as fearless as he is. Straight through thorn bushes, over big rocks and broken ground, and under overhanging branches we went, my uneasy thoughts racing ahead of us. And then as we crashed into a patch of twelve-foot-high *nal* grass the elephant hesitated before going on again, and Ajmat leant back and whispered, 'She can smell the tiger, so hold tight Sahib, for you are unarmed.' Only another hundred yards to go now, and as yet no signal had come from the guns, each of whom had been provided with a railwayman's whistle with instructions to blow it if help was needed. But the fact that no whistle had sounded gave me no comfort for I knew from past experience that in times of excitement even bigger things than whistles can be dropped from a *machan*. And then through the trees I caught sight of Joan and could have shouted with joy and relief, for she was unconcernedly sitting on her *machan* with her rifle across her knees. On seeing me she spread her arms wide—which I rightly interpreted as meaning a big tiger—and then pointed down in front of Bunty's *machan*.

The rest of the story, which makes my heart miss a beat as I relate it even after this lapse of fifteen years, is soon told; a story which, but for the courage of three young people and superlative marksmanship, would have ended in a terrible tragedy.

Our shout when I started the beat was clearly heard by the guns, also the faint clapping of our hands. Then in the interval the tiger broke cover sixty yards in front of *machan* No. 3, and came slowly along the game-track. It reached the foot of the bank as we on the elephants shouted the second time. On hearing this shout the tiger stopped and looked over its shoulder. Satisfied that there was no need to hurry, it stood listening for a minute or so, and then started up the bank. When it reached the spot where I had laid a dry stick across the track, Bunty fired, but she fired at its chest, for the tiger was holding its head low and she could not see its throat. On receiving the shot, which was well placed, and before either Bunty or Peter was able to get in a second shot, the tiger sprang forward with a roar and attacked the *machan* from underneath. While the frail *machan* was rocking on the stunted tree and threatening to disintegrate under the onslaught of the tiger, and while Bunty and Peter were trying desperately to push the muzzles of their rifles through the floor of the *machan*, Joan, from her *machan* thirty yards away, knocked the tiger down with her first shot and as it fell to the ground put a second bullet into it. On receiving Joan's second bullet the tiger started to go down the bank, evidently with the intention of regaining the thick cover it had just left, and Bunty then put a bullet through the back of its head.

That was our Viceroy's first visit to Kaladhungi, but it was not his last, and during the many subsequent occasions on which he honoured our small foothill village with his presence I never had one moment's anxiety for his safety, or for the safety of those who accompanied him. For I never again took risks such as I took on the last day of that memorable shoot.

chapter eleven

FROM NOVEMBER TO MARCH THE climate of the Himalayan foothills has no equal, and the best of these five months is February. In February the air is crisp and invigorating and the wealth of bird life that migrated down from the high mountains in November, in search of food and of warmth, is still with us. The deciduous trees that have stood gaunt and naked throughout the autumn and winter are bursting into bloom, or are putting on a mantle of tender leaf buds of varying shades of green or pink. In February spring is in the very air, in the sap of all trees, and in the blood of all wild life. Whether it be on the mountains in the north, or the plains in the south, or in the shelter of the foothills, spring comes in a night. It is winter when you go to bed one night and when you awaken next morning it is spring, and round you all nature is rejoicing in anticipation of the pleasures that

lie ahead, plentiful food, warmth, and the reproduction of life.
The migrant birds are packing into small groups, these groups
will join others, and on the appointed day and at the command
of the leaders the pigeons, paroquets, thrushes, and other fruit-
eaters will fly up the valleys to their selected nesting grounds
while insect-eaters flitting from tree to tree in the same direction
and on the same quest will cover at most a few miles a day.
While the migrants are preparing for departure and the regular
inhabitants of the foothills are selecting each his own mate and
looking for a building site, the combined population of the
jungle are vying with each other in a vocal contest which starts
at daylight and continues non-stop until dark. In this contest
all take part even to the predatory birds whose most vocal
member, the serpent eagle, while showing as a mere
speck against the blue sky sends his piercing
cry back to earth.

While instructing troops in jungle warfare I was
in a forest one day in Central India with a party of
men among whom were several bird enthusiasts.
High in the heavens above us a serpent eagle was
circling and screaming. The party was a new draft
from different parts of the United Kingdom,
destined for Burma, none of whom had ever seen
a serpent eagle. Waiting until we came to an open
glade I pointed to a speck in the sky. Field-glasses were
produced and disappointment was expressed at the bird
being too far away to identify or to see clearly. Telling my
companions to stand quite still I took a three-
inch-long reed from my pocket, and sounded a
note on it. This reed, split at one end and
blocked up at the other, reproduced with great
exactitude the piercing call of a young deer

in distress and was used in my training for signalling, for it is the only natural sound to be heard—both by day and by night—in jungles in which there are deer, and it was, therefore, a sound least likely to attract the attention of an enemy. On hearing the sound the eagle stopped screaming, for though a serpent eagle, living principally on snakes, he does not despise other flesh. Closing his wings he dropped a few hundred feet and then again started soaring in circles. At each call he came nearer, until finally he was circling just above tree-top level where the party with me had a close and clear view of him. Do those who were in that party of fifty, and who survived the Burma campaign, remember that day in the Chindwara jungles and your disappointment at my not being able to make the eagle perch on a branch close enough to photograph? Never mind. Accompany me now on this spring morning and we will see many things just as interesting as that serpent eagle.

You have travelled far on the road of knowledge since that distant Chindwara day. Self-preservation has taught you that the human eye has a field of vision of 180 degrees. Pin-pointing sound which at first you found so difficult is now second nature to you. And having learnt when a boy the difference between the smell of a rose and of a violet you can now identify each tree and plant by the smell of its flower even when that flower is at tree-top level, or hidden deep in the jungle. But much as you have learnt and greatly as the knowledge has added to your confidence, safety, and pleasure, much still remains to learn and on this beautiful spring morning we will add a little to our store of knowledge.

The canal that forms the northern boundary of our estate, and in which the girls used to bathe, is conveyed across the watercourse I have previously referred to by an aqueduct. This aqueduct is known as *Bijli Dant*, which means, 'lightning water channel'. The original aqueduct built by Sir Henry Ramsay was destroyed by lightning many years ago, and because of a local superstition that lightning is attracted to a given spot by an evil spirit, usually in the form of a snake, the old foundations were not used and a parallel aqueduct was built that has been functioning now for half a century. Wild animals that visit the village at night from the jungles to the north, and who do not like wading or jumping the ten-foot-wide canal, pass under the aqueduct. So on this spring morning we will start our walk from this point.

On the sand in the passage-way under the arch of the aqueduct are the tracks of hare, *kakar*, pig, porcupine, hyaena, and jackal. Of these the only tracks we will look closely at are the tracks of the porcupine, for, having been made after the night wind had died down, they are free of drift sand. Five toes and a pad and each footprint is distinct, for a porcupine has no need to stalk and does not superimpose one foot upon another. In front of each print is a small hole in the sand made by the porcupine's strong nails, on which he depends to a great extent for his food. The hind pads of porcupines are elongated. This projection, or heel, is not as marked as it is in the case of bear. It is, however, sufficiently marked to distinguish the track of a porcupine from the tracks of all other animals. If you want further confirmation, look closely at the track and you will see a number of finely-drawn lines running between, or parallel to, the track. These finely drawn lines are made by the long drooping quills of the porcupine when they make contact with the ground. A porcupine cannot cast or project its quills, which are barbed, and its method of defence or attack is to raise its quills on end

and run backwards. At the end of a porcupine's tail are a number of hollow quills, not unlike long wine glasses on slender stems. These quills are used as a rattle to intimidate enemies, and to convey water to the porcupine's burrow. The quills readily fill with water when submerged, and the porcupine uses this water to keep its burrow cool and free of dust. Porcupines are vegetarians and live on fruit, roots, and field-crops. They also consume the horns shed by deer and the horns of deer killed by leopards, wild dogs, and tigers, possibly to obtain calcium or some other vitamin absent in their normal food. Though a comparatively small animal a porcupine has a big heart, and he will defend himself against great odds.

For a few hundred yards above the aqueduct the bed of the watercourse is stony and, except where a game-track crosses it, we shall find no more tracks until we come to a long stretch of fine silt, washed down from the foothills, on which the tracks of all the animals that use the watercourse as a highway show up clearly. This stretch of ground is flanked on either side by dense *lantana* in which deer, pig, peafowl, and jungle-fowl, shelter during daylight hours and into which only leopards, tigers, and porcupines venture at night. In the *lantana* you can now hear jungle-fowl scratching up the dead leaves, and a hundred yards away on the topmost branch of a leafless *samal* tree is perched their most deadly enemy, a crested eagle. The eagle is not only the enemy of jungle-fowl, he is also the enemy of peafowl. These are his natural prey and the fact that there are as many old birds as young ones in the jungle, is proof that they are able to look after themselves. For this reason I never interfered with crested eagles until one day, on hearing the distressed cry of a young deer, I hurried to the spot and found a crested eagle holding down a month-old *cheetal* fawn and tearing at its head, while the distracted mother ran round in circles striking at the bird with her forefeet. Desperately as the brave mother had tried to rescue her young one—and of this the scratches and blood on her muzzle bore ample proof—the great eagle had been too much for her, and though I was able to dispose of her enemy I was unable to do anything for her young, beyond putting it out of its misery, for even if I had been able to heal its wounds I would not have been able to restore its sight. That incident has cost the lives of many crested eagles in the jungles in which I have hunted, for though it is difficult to approach close enough to shoot them with a shotgun, they offer a good target for an accurate rifle. The bird on the *samal* tree, however, has nothing to fear from us for we have come out to see things, and not to deal with the enemies of young deer. In my catapult days the greatest battle in which a crested eagle has ever been engaged took place on a stretch of sand, in the bed of the river, a little below the Boar bridge. Possibly mistaking a fish cat for a hare the eagle stooped on it and either because he was unable to withdraw

his talons, or because he lost his temper, became involved in a life-and-death struggle. Both contestants were equally well armed for the battle; the cat with its teeth and claws, and the eagle with its beak and talons. It is greatly to be regretted that photography at that time was confined to studios and movie cameras were unknown, and that no record was made of that long-drawn-out and desperate battle. If a cat has nine lives an eagle has ten, and it was lives that ultimately proved the deciding factor. With one precarious life still in hand the eagle left his dead opponent on the sand, and trailing a broken wing went down to a pool in the river where, after quenching his thirst, he surrendered his tenth life.

Several game-tracks lead on to the open ground from the *lantana* and while we have been looking at the eagle a young kakar stag has walked out of the *lantana* on to the watercourse, fifty yards away, with the intention of crossing it. If we freeze and remain frozen, he will take no notice of us. Of all the animals in the jungle the *kakar* gives the impression of being most on his toes. Even here on this open ground he is walking on tiptoe with his hind legs tucked well under him and at the first indication of danger, be it conveyed by sight, sound, or smell, he will dash away at top speed. The *kakar* is sometimes described as being a mean and a cowardly little animal, and unreliable as a jungle informant. With this description I do not agree. No animal can be called mean for that is exclusively a human trait, and no animal that lives in the densest jungles with tigers, as the *kakar* does, can be accused of being a coward. As for being an unreliable informant I know of no better friend that a man who shoots on foot can have in a jungle than a *kakar*. He is small and defenceless and his enemies are many, and if in a beat he barks at a python or at a pine-marten, when he is expected to bark only at a tiger, he is more to be pitied than accused of being unreliable. For to him and his kind, these two ruthless enemies are a very real menace and he is only carrying out his function— as a watcher—when he warns the jungle folk of their presence.

The *kakar* has two long canine teeth or tusks on its upper jaw. These tusks are very sharp and are the *kakar's* only means of defence, for the points of his short horns are curved inwards and are of little use as weapons of defence. Some years ago there was a long and inconclusive correspondence in the Indian press about a peculiar sound that *kakar* make on occasions. This sound can best be described as a clicking sound, resembling that made by the bones used by Christy minstrels. It was asserted by some that, as the sound was only heard when *kakar* were running, it was caused by double joints, and by others that it was caused by the tusks being clashed together in some unexplained way. Both these assertions, and others that were advanced, were incorrect. The sound is made by the animal's mouth in exactly the same way as all other vocal sounds are made, and is used on various occasions: as, for instance, when uncertain of a seen object, when disturbed by a gun dog, or when pursuing a mate. The alarm call of the *kakar* is a clear ringing bark, resembling that of a medium-sized dog.

While the *kakar* has been crossing the watercourse a large flight of insect and fruit-eating birds has approached us from our right. In this flight are migrants as well as local inhabitants, and if we stand where we are the birds will fly over our heads and you will have an opportunity of studying them as they perch on the trees and bushes on both sides of the watercourse, and also while they are in flight. Birds, except when they are very close, are difficult to identify by their colours when sitting where they have no background or when seen against the sky, but every species of bird can be identified while in flight by its shape and by its wing beats. In the flight that is approaching us, every member of which is either chirping, twittering, or whistling, are two varieties of minivets, the short-billed scarlet, and the small orange-breasted. Minivets perch on the topmost leaves and twigs of trees and bushes, and from these commanding positions keep darting into the air to catch winged insects disturbed by their own kind or by other members of the flight. With the minivets are:

Six varieties of tits. The grey, yellow-cheeked, blue-winged, red-billed, white-eyed, and the common green.

Four varieties of flycatchers. The white-browed fantail, yellow fantail, slaty-headed, and verditer.

Six varieties of woodpeckers. The golden-backed, black-naped green, rufous-bellied pied, pigmy pied, yellow-naped, and the scaly-bellied green.

Four varieties of bulbuls. The golden-fronted green, white-winged green, white-cheeked crested, and the red-whiskered.

Three varieties of sunbirds. The Himalayan red, purple, and the small green.

In addition to these birds, which number between two and three hundred, there are a pair of black-headed golden orioles who are chasing each other from tree to tree, and a lesser racket-tailed drongo who, though not as aggressive as his big brother, has nevertheless acquired several juicy morsels from the flight he is guarding, the last being a fat larva industriously dug out of a dry branch by the pigmy pied woodpecker. The flight of birds has now flown over our heads and disappeared into the jungle on our left, and the only sound to be heard is the scratching of the jungle-fowl in the *lantana*, and the only bird to be seen is the crested eagle, patient and hopeful, on the topmost branch of the *samal* tree.

Beyond the *lantana* on the right is an open stretch of parklike ground, on which grow a number of big plum trees. From this direction now comes the alarm bark of a red monkey, followed a few seconds later by the excited chattering and barking of fifty or more monkeys of varying ages and sizes. A leopard is on the move and as he is on more or less open ground it is unlikely that he is trying to secure a kill, in which case he is possibly making for one or other of the deep ravines in the foothills where leopards are often to be found during the hot hours of the day. Winding through the plum trees is a path used both by human beings and by animals. This path crosses our watercourse two hundred yards farther on and as there is a good chance, I would almost say a certainty, of the leopard coming along the path,

let us hurry forward for a hundred and fifty yards and sit down
with our backs against the high bank on the left. The watercourse
here is fifty yards wide and on the trees on the left-hand side is
a large troupe of *langurs*. The warning given by the red monkeys
has been heeded, and all the mothers in the troupe have got
hold of their young ones, and all eyes are turned in the direction
from which the warning came.

There is no need for you to keep your eyes on the path, for
the young *langur* who is sitting out on the extreme end of a
branch on the tree nearest the path will give us warning of the
leopard's approach. *Langurs* act differently
from red monkeys on seeing a leopard. This
may be due to better organization, or to
their being less courageous than their red
cousins. All the red monkeys in a troupe
will chatter and bark at the same time on
seeing a leopard, and where the jungle is
suitable they will follow it over the treetops for considerable distances. The *langurs*
act differently. When the young look-out
sees the leopard he will give the alarm call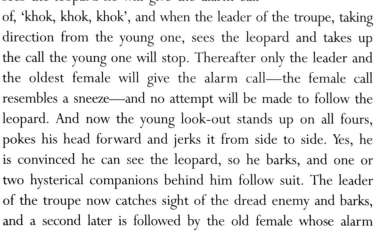
of, 'khok, khok, khok', and when the leader of the troupe, taking
direction from the young one, sees the leopard and takes up
the call the young one will stop. Thereafter only the leader and
the oldest female will give the alarm call—the female call
resembles a sneeze—and no attempt will be made to follow the
leopard. And now the young look-out stands up on all fours,
pokes his head forward and jerks it from side to side. Yes, he
is convinced he can see the leopard, so he barks, and one or
two hysterical companions behind him follow suit. The leader
of the troupe now catches sight of the dread enemy and barks,
and a second later is followed by the old female whose alarm

call, 'tch', resembles a sneeze. The young ones are now silent and confine themsleves to bobbing their heads up and down, and making faces. The troupe appear to know instinctively that they have nothing to fear from the leopard on this spring morning, for if he had been hungry and out to kill he would not have walked out on to the open watercourse as he has done, but would have crossed either higher up or lower down, and approached them unseen. Being as agile, and little heavier, the leopard experiences no difficulty in catching *langurs*. But it is different with red monkeys, for they retire to the extremities of thin branches, where the leopard is afraid to trust his weight.

With head held high, and the morning sun shining on his beautifully marked coat, the leopard is now crossing the fifty yards of open ground, paying not the slightest attention to the *langurs* clustered on the trees he is approaching. Once he stops, and after looking up and down the watercourse without noticing us as we sit motionless with our backs to the bank, he continues unhurriedly on his way. Climbing the steep bank he disappears from our view, but as long as he is in sight of the leader and of the old female they will continue to send their warning call into the jungle.

Let us now examine the tracks of the leopard. The path where it crosses the watercourse runs over red clay, trodden hard by bare human feet. Over this clay is a coating of fine white dust, so the conditions for our purpose are ideal. We will assume that we did not see the leopard, and that we have come on the tracks by accident. The first thing we note is that the pug marks have every appearance of having been newly made, and therefore that they are fresh. We get this impression from the fact that the pile or nap of the dust where it took the weight of the leopard is laid flat and smooth, and that the walls of the dust surrounding the pads and toes are clear cut and more or less perpendicular.

Presently under the action of the wind and the rays of the hot sun the nap will stand up again and the walls will begin to crumble. Ants and other insects will cross the track; dust will drift into it; bits of grass and dead leaves will be blown on to, or will fall on it; and in time the pug marks will be obliterated. There is no hard-and-fast rule by which you can judge the age of a track, whether it be the pug marks of a leopard or tiger, or the track of a snake or a deer. But by close observation and by taking into consideration the position of the track, whether in an exposed or in a sheltered spot, the time of day and of night when certain insects are on the move, the time at which winds normally blow, and the time at which dew begins to fall or to drip from the trees, you can make a more or less accurate guess when the track was made. In the present case we have satisfied ourselves from the appearance of the track that it is fresh, but this is not the only interesting point about it. We have yet to determine whether the leopard was a male or a female, whether it was old or young, and whether it was a big or a small animal. The round shape of the pug marks show it was a male. The absence of any cracks or creases in the pads, the round toes, and compact appearance of the entire pug marks show that the leopard was young. With regard to size, here again only observation and experience will enable you to judge the size of animals by their pug marks, and when you have gained this experience you can assess the length of either a leopard or a tiger to a possible error of an inch or two. The Koals of Mirzapur, when asked the size of a tiger, measure the pug mark with a blade of grass and then, laying the blade down, measure it with the width of their fingers. How accurate their method is I am not in a position to say. For myself I prefer to guess the size or length of an animal from the general appearance of its pug mark, for whatever method is adopted, it can at best be only a guess.

A little beyond where the path crosses the watercourse there is a narrow strip of firm sand, flanked on one side by rocks and on the other by a high bank. A herd of *cheetal* has gone along this strip of sand. It is always interesting when in a jungle to count the number of animals in a herd, whether *cheetal* or *sambhar*, and to take note of the individual members. This enables you to recognize the herd when you next see it and to assess casualties, and, further, it gives you a friendly feeling towards the herd as being one that you know. If the herd is on open ground it is not difficult to count the stags, note the length and shape of their horns, and count the hinds and young ones. When, however, only one of the herd is visible and the others are in cover, the following method of inducing the hidden animals to come out into the open will, nine times out of ten, be found effective. After stalking to within a reasonable distance of the deer you can see, lie down behind a tree or a bush and give the call of a leopard. All animals can pin-point sound, and when the deer is looking in your direction project your shoulder a little beyond the bole of the tree, and move it slowly up and down once or twice, or shake a few leaves of the bush. On seeing the movement the deer will start calling; and its companions will leave the cover and range themselves on either side of her. I have on occasion got as many as fifty *cheetal* to show themselves in this way to enable me to photograph them at leisure. I would like, however, to add one word of warning. Never try calling like a leopard, or any other animal, unless you are absolutely certain you have the area to yourself, and even then keep a careful look all round. The following is my reason for the warning. I heard a leopard calling repeatedly one night, and from the intonation of the call I concluded it was in distress. Before daylight next morning I set off to try to find out, if I could, what was wrong with the animal. During the night it had changed its position and I now located it on a hill some distance away, where it was still calling. Selecting a spot where a game-track led on to an open glade, and where I would see the leopard before it saw me, I lay down behind a boundary pillar and answered the call. Thereafter, for a matter of half an hour or more, call answered call. The leopard was coming but it was slow about it and was coming very cautiously. Eventually when it was a hundred yards away I stopped calling. I was lying flat down with my elbows resting on the ground and my chin resting in my hands, momentarily expecting the leopard to appear, when I heard the swish of leaves behind me and on turning my head, looked straight into the muzzle of a rifle. Late the previous evening Cassels, Deputy Commissioner of Naini Tal, and Colonel Ward had arrived at the forest bungalow and unknown to me had shot a leopard cub. During the night the mother had been heard calling and at crack of dawn Ward set out on an elephant to try to shoot the mother. Dew was on the ground, and the mahout was well trained, and he brought his elephant up without a sound until only a fringe of trees lay between us. Ward could see me, but he was not as young as he had been and, further, the early morning light was not too good, and he was unable to get the sights of his rifle to bear accurately on my shoulders, so he signalled the elephant to go forward. Mercifully for all of us, when the elephant cleared the fringe of trees and was only ten yards from me, and when the mahout—also an old man—was pointing and Ward was leaning down and aligning his sights for a second time the elephant released a branch it was holding down, and, hearing the sound, I turned my head and looked up into the muzzle of a heavy rifle.

The herd of *cheetal* whose tracks we are looking at and in which we are now interested, went along the strip of sand the previous evening. This you can tell from the night insects that have crossed the tracks, and from the dew drops that have fallen on them from an overhanging tree. The herd may be a mile or five miles away, out on an open glade or hidden in cover; even so, we will count the number of animals in the herd and this I will show you how to do. We will assume that when a *cheetal* is standing, the distance between its hind- and fore-hooves is thirty inches. Take a stick and draw a line across the sand at right angles to the tracks. Measure thirty inches from the line you have drawn, this will be easy for your shoes are ten inches long, and draw a second line across the sand parallel to the first. Now take your stick and count the number of hoof prints between the two lines, marking each print with the point of your stick as you do so. The result of your count is, let us say, thirty. Divide this number by two and you can be *reasonably* sure that there were fifteen *cheetal* in the herd that passed that way the previous evening. This method of counting animals of any species, whether wild or domestic, will give accurate results for small numbers, say up to ten, and approximate results for greater numbers, provided the distance between the hind- and fore-feet is known. In the case of small animals such as wild dogs, pigs, and sheep, the distance will be less than thirty inches, and in the case of large animals such as *sambhar* and domestic cattle it will be more than thirty inches.

For the information of those who were not with me during the years of training for jungle warfare, I should like to assert that it is possible to glean a lot of useful information from the footprints of human beings in a jungle, whether seen on a road, path, or game-track, or in fact anywhere where the footprints of men in motion are to be seen. Let us assume, for the sake of interest, that we are in enemy country and that we have come on a game-track on which there are footprints. From the appearance of the footprints, their size, shape, absence or presence of nails or sprags, iron shod or plain heels, leather soles or rubber, and so on, we conclude that the prints have not been made by members of our own force, but by the enemy. This point being settled we have to determine when the party passed that way, and the number of men in the party. You know how to assess the time. To find out the number of men in the party we will draw a line across the track, and with the toe of one foot on this line take a step of thirty inches, and draw a second line across the track. The number of heel marks between these two lines will give the number of men in the party. There are other interesting things you can learn from the footprints, and one of the most important of these is the speed at which the party was travelling. When a human being is moving at a normal pace his weight is distributed evenly over his footprint and his stride is from thirty to thirty-two inches, according to his height. As the speed is increased less weight falls on the heel and more on the toes, the imprint of the heel gets less and the imprint of the toes greater, and the length of the stride gets longer. This process of less heel and more toes continues to get more apparent until when running at full speed little more than the ball of the foot and the toes come in contact with the ground. If the party was a small one, ten or a dozen in all, it will be possible to see if any were limping, and blood on the track will indicate that one or more were wounded.

If you ever get a flesh wound in the jungles I will show you a small and insignificant little plant that will not only cauterize but also heal your wound better than anything else that I know. The plant, which is found in all jungles, grows to a height of twelve inches, and has a daisylike flower on a long slender stem. The leaves are fleshy and serrated, like the leaf of a chrysanthemum. To use the plant break off a few leaves, rinse them in water to wash off the dust—if water is available—and then squeeze the leaves between finger and thumb, and pour the juice freely into the wound. No further treatment is needed and, if the wound is not a deep one, it will heal in a day or two. The plant is well named, *Brahm Buti*, 'God's flower'.

Many of you were my good comrades in the Indian and Burma jungles during the war years and if I worked you hard, because time was short, you will long since have forgiven me. And I hope you have not forgotten all that we learnt together, as for instance: the fruit and flowers it was safe to eat; where to look for edible roots and tubers; the best substitutes for tea and coffee; what plants, barks, and leaves to use for fever, sores, and sore throats; what barks and creepers to use for stretchers, and for making ropes to sling heavy equipment and guns across streams and ravines; how to avoid getting trench feet and prickly heat; how to create fire; how to obtain dry fuel in a wet forest; how to kill game without resort to fire-arms; how to cook or make a dish of tea without metal utensils; how to procure a substitute for salt; how to treat snake bites, wounds, and stomach disorders. And, finally, how to keep fit and conduct ourselves in the jungles to live at peace with all wildlife. These and many other things you and I, from the mountains and plains of India, from the villages and cities of the United Kingdom, from the United States of America, from Canada, Australia, New Zealand, and from other lands, learned together. Not with the object of spending the rest of our days in the jungles, but to give us confidence in ourselves and in each other, to remove our fears of the unknown, and to show our enemies that you were better men than they. But much as we learned in those days of good comradeship we only touched the fringe of knowledge, for the book of nature has no end as it has no beginning.

We have still much of our spring morning before us, and we have now arrived at the foothills where the vegetation differs from that on the flat ground we have recently traversed. Here there are a number of ficus and plum trees that have attracted a variety of fruit-eating birds, the most interesting of which are the giant hornbills. Hornbills nest in hollow trees and have the unusual habit of sealing the females into the nests. This habit throws a heavy burden on the male, for the female moults and grows enormously fat during the incubation period and when the eggs—usually two—are hatched she is unable to fly, and the male has the strenuous task of providing food for the whole family. By his ungainly appearance, his enormous beak fitted with a sound-box, and his heavy and laboured flight, the hornbill gives the impression of having missed the bus of evolution. And his habit of sealing up the nest and leaving only a small hole through which the female projects the tip of her beak to take the food the male brings her, possibly dates back to prehistoric days when the bird had more powerful enemies than it has today. All birds that nest in hollow trees or that make holes in trees in which to nest, have common enemies. Some of these birds— tits, robins, hoopoes—are quite defenceless and the question therefore arises why the hornbill, who by reason of its powerful beak is best able to defend itself, should be the only one of these many tree-nesting birds to consider it necessary to seal up its nest. Another unusual habit which the hornbill does not share with any other bird that I know of, is its habit of adorning its feathers with pigment. This pigment, which is yellow and can be readily wiped off with a handkerchief, is carried in a small sack above the tail and is laid with the beak on to two broad white bands that extend across the width of the wings. Why the hornbill finds it necessary to paint these white bands yellow with a pigment that washes off every time it rains, I can only attribute to camouflage against an enemy, or enemies, that it suffered from in bygone days. For the only enemy it occasionally suffers from now is a leopard, and against a leopard operating at night camouflage is of little avail.

In addition to the hornbills there are a number of other fruit-eating birds on the ficus and plum trees. Among these are two varieties of green pigeon, the Bengal, and the pintail. Two varieties of barbet, the crimson-breasted, and the common green. Four varieties of *bulbul*, the Himalayan black, common Bengal, red-whiskered, and white-cheeked. Three varieties of paroquets, the rose-ringed, the Alexandrine, and the blossom-

headed. Scratching among the dead leaves and eating the ripe fruit dropped by the other birds, are fifty or more white-capped laughing thrushes. These thrushes were the last to migrate from the high nesting-grounds and will be the first to return to them.

Near the ficus trees is a fire-track, and crossing it is a well-worn game-track which runs straight up the hill to a salt-lick near which there is a saucer of water fed by a tiny spring. Between the salt-lick and the water is an old stump. Here a stunted *kusum* tree stood, in the branches of which poachers repeatedly built *machans*. Shooting over salt-licks and over water is prohibited, but poachers are no respecters of game laws, and as dismantling the *machans* had no effect I eventually cut the tree down. I have heard it stated that carnivora do not kill at salt-licks and water holes. However considerate carnivora may be in other parts of the world, in India they certainly have no compunction about killing at salt-licks. In fact it is at these places that they do most of their killing, as you can see from the bones and the horns partly eaten by porcupines that you will find in the vicinity of this salt-lick, and in the vicinity of all salt-licks that are surrounded by forests in which deer and monkeys live.

Let us now climb the hill above the salt-lick to a point from where we can get a bird's eye view of the foothills and the forests that lie at their feet. Before us stretches the forest through which we have just come to our starting-point, the canal. This forest is as nature made it, for it has little timber of commercial value and has, therefore, escaped the devastating hand of man. The light green patches in the foreground are *shisham* saplings which have grown from seeds washed down from the foothills by monsoon floods. Later, when these saplings grow to maturity, they will provide the best timber for cart wheels, and for furniture. The dark-green patches with clusters of red berries are runi trees, which provide the powder known to commerce as *kamala*. When the poor people who migrate in winter from the high hills to the foothills in search of food and warmth—as do the birds—can spare a day from their regular labours, old and young

resort to the jungles to collect *kamala*. *Kamala* is a red powder
which adheres to the *runi* berry, and the method of collection
is to cut down the branches, strip the berries into big shallow
baskets, and then with the hand rub the berries against the sides
of the basket. The powder when freed from the berries drifts
through the cracks in the basket and is caught on a *cheetal* skin,
or square of cloth. A family of five—a man and his wife and
three children—working from sunrise to sunset can, when the
crop is plentiful, collect four pounds of powder worth from one
to two rupees, according to the market price. The powder is
used in India and the Middle East for dyeing wool, and until
dishonest middlemen started adulterating *kamala* with brick dust,
it was extensively used in the United States for colouring butter.
The powder is also used for medicinal purposes, and mustard oil
in which *runi* berries have been boiled is used for rheumatism.

Interspersed with the *shisham* saplings and *runi* trees, are
feathery-leaved *khair* trees. These *khair* trees in addition to
providing the foothill villages with plowshares, provide a cottage
industry for tens of thousands of poor people in the United
Provinces. The industry, which is a winter one and is carried on
day and night for a period of four months, produces a commodity
known locally as *kach*, and to commerce as catechu. It also
produces—as a by-product—the dye known as khaki, used for
dyeing cloth and fishing nets. A friend of mine, a man by the
name of Mirza, was, I believe, the first to discover khaki dye,
and the discovery was accidental. Mirza was one day leaning over
an iron pan in which *khair* chips were being boiled, to make
kach, when a white handkerchief he was carrying fell into the
pan. Fishing the handkerchief out with a stick Mirza sent it to
the wash. When the handkerchief was brought back Mirza found
it had not lost any of its colour, so, reprimanding the washerman,
he told him to take it away and clean it. Returning with the

handkerchief the washerman said he had tried every method known to his trade of removing stains, but he could not take the colour out of the small square of linen. It was thus that Mirza found he had discovered a fast dye, which is now produced in the flourishing factory he erected at Izattnagar.

Mingled with the many shades of green—for each tree has its own individual colour—are vivid splashes of orange, gold, lilac, pink, and red. The trees with orange coloured flowers are *dhank* (Butea Giondosa) which produces a ruby-coloured gum used for dyeing silk of the finest quality. The trees with the three-foot-long showers of golden bloom are *amaltas* (Cassia Fistula). The two-foot-long cylindrical seedpods of this tree contain a sweet jelly like substance which is used throughout Kumaon as a laxative. The trees with the big lilac coloured flowers are *kachanar* (Bauhinia). The pink are *kusum* trees and the mass of pink shading from delicate shell to deep rose, are not flowers but tender young leaves. The red are *samal* (silk cotton) trees the flowers of which are loved by all birds that drink nectar, and by paroquets and monkeys that eat the fleshy flowers, and by deer and pigs that eat them when they fall to the ground. Later in the year the *samal* flowers will give way to large woody seedpods. When the hot winds blow in April these pods will explode like anti-aircraft shells and a white cloud of silk cotton (kapoc used in life-belts), each section carrying a seed, will drift away in the wind to regenerate nature's garden. All seeds that are not carried from one place to another by birds or animals are provided with buoyant material or with parchment sails or propellers, to enable the winds of heaven to carry them from place to place. There are, of course, exceptions, one of which is the gotail which bears a fruit like a small green apple and which no bird or animal eats. This tree grows on the banks of rivers and the water does for its seeds what birds and animals, and the wind, do for other seeds.

Another is the coconut, which is provided with a husk that enables it to float and be carried by the ocean waves from shore to shore.

Beyond the canal, our starting-point, is our village. The vivid green and gold patches show where the young wheat is sprouting, and where the mustard crop is in full flower. The white line at the foot of the village is the boundary wall, which took ten years to build, and beyond the wall the forest stretches in an unbroken line until it merges into the horizon. To the east and to the west as far as the eye can see is limitless forest, and behind us the hills rise ridge upon ridge to the eternal snows.

Here as we sit in this beautiful and peaceful spot in the shadow of the mighty Himalayas, with the forest round us putting on a new mantle of spring, with every current of wind bringing with it the sweet smell of flowers, and with the air throbbing with the joyful songs of a great multitude of birds, we can forget for a spell the strains and stresses of our world, and savour the world of the jungle folk. For here the law of the jungle prevails. The law that

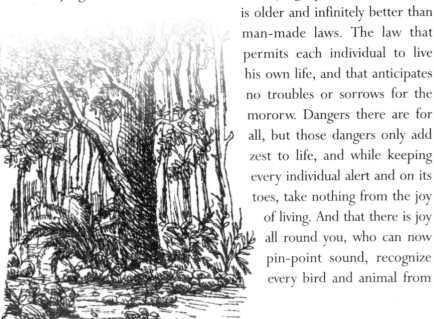

is older and infinitely better than man-made laws. The law that permits each individual to live his own life, and that anticipates no troubles or sorrows for the mororw. Dangers there are for all, but those dangers only add zest to life, and while keeping every individual alert and on its toes, take nothing from the joy of living. And that there is joy all round you, who can now pin-point sound, recognize every bird and animal from

its call, and assign a reason for the call, have ample proof. Away
to our left a peacock is screaming his mating call and from that
call you know he is dancing, with tail-feathers spread, to impress
a bevy of admiring hens. Nearer at hand a jungle-cock is crowing
defiance to all and sundry and is being answered by others of
his kind who are equally defiant. But of fights there are few, for
to fight in the jungle exposes the contestants to danger. Away
to our right a *sambhar* stag is warning the jungle folk that the
leopard we saw an hour ago is lying out on an exposed spot
basking in the sun. The stag will bell until the leopard retires
for the day into heavy cover, where he will be screened from the
prying eyes of informants. In a thicket below us twenty or more
white-eyed tits, white-winged bulbuls, and grey headed flycatchers,
have found a spotted owlet dozing in a leafy bower and are
calling to companions to come and see what they have found.
They know it is safe to approach and scream into the wise one's
very ears, for only when he has young will he occasionally kill
in daylight. And the owlet on his part knows that no matter how
much he is feared and hated by his tormentors, he has nothing
to fear from them, and that when they tire of their sport they
will leave him to his sleep. In the air all round there is sound,
and each sound has a meaning. The liquid notes, the most
beautiful of all the songs to be heard in our jungles, is a *shama*
wooing a bashful mate. The tap-tap-tapping is a golden-backed
woodpecker making a hole in a dead tree for his new home.
The harsh braying is a *cheetal* stag challenging a rival to battle.
High in the heavens a serpent eagle is screaming, and higher
still a flight of vultures are patiently quartering the sky. Yesterday,
first a Himalyan blue magpie, and then a pair of crows, showed
the vultures where a tiger had hidden his kill in a thicket near
where the peacock is now dancing, and today as they circle and
soar they are hoping for the same good fortune.

As you sit here, alone or in company with a friend, you can realize to the full what your knowledge of jungle lore means to you, and how greatly that knowledge has added to your confidence and to your pleasure. No longer does the jungle hold any terrors for you, for you know there is nothing for you to be afraid of. If the necessity arose you could live on the jungles, and you could lie down whereever you were and sleep without any feeling of unease. You have learnt to maintain direction, to be conscious at all times of wind direction, and you will never again lose yourself in the jungle no matter whether you move by night or by day. Hard though it was at first to train your eyes, you know now that your field of vision is 180 degrees and that every movement in that field will be seen by you. You can enter into the lives of all the jungle folk, for you have learnt their language; and being able to locate sound, you can follow their every movement. You can now move silently, and shoot accurately, and if the necessity ever arose again for you to face an enemy in the jungles you would not face him with an inferiority complex, but with the full knowledge that no matter what his reputation you are a better-trained man than he is, and have nothing to learn or to fear from him.

It is now time to wend our way home, for we have a long way to go, and Maggie will be waiting breakfast for us. We will return the way we came and as we pass the strip of sand on which we counted the *cheetal* tracks, the path by which the leopard crossed the watercourse, the fine silt washed down from the foothills, and the passage-way under the aqueduct, we will drag a branch behind us. This we will do to obliterate our tracks, and all the tracks we saw this morning so that when we visit the jungle again tomorrow, the next day, or maybe the day after, we will know that all the tracks we see date from the time we last passed that way.

chapter twelve

WHILE ABSORBING JUNGLE LORE IT is possible to develop a sense that has been handed down to us from the days of primitive man and which, for want of a better name, I shall call, Jungle Sensitiveness. This sense, which can be acquired only by living in the jungles in close association with wild life, is the development of the subconscious warning of danger.

Many individuals can testify to having avoided trouble by acting on an impulse that came how they knew not, and that warned their subconscious being against an impending danger. In one case the warning may have been against proceeding along a certain street in which a moment later a bomb exploded; in another, moving just in time from the vicinity of a building wrecked a second later by a shell; or in yet another, stepping away from the shelter of a tree which a moment later was struck by lightning.

Whatever the danger may have been that the impulse enabled the individual to avoid, it was a *known* and an *anticipated* danger. In the story of the Chowgarh man-eater I have given two instances of subconscious warning. At the time the warning was conveyed to me the whole of my attention was concentrated on avoiding being killed by the man-eater, and the warning I received that danger of an attack from a man-eater threatened—in the one case from a piled-up heap of rocks, and in the other from an overhanging rock under which I had to pass—was therefore quite natural and understandable. I should now like to give one instance of *unconscious* warning of *unsuspected* danger, which I can only explain as resulting from highly developed jungle sensitiveness.

It was my custom during the winter months at Kaladhungi to shoot an occasional *sambhar* or *cheetal* stag for the tenants of our village. One afternoon a deputation arrived to remind me that I had shot no meat for some time, and to request me to shoot a *cheetal* to celebrate a local festival on the morrow. The jungles were very dry at the time, making stalking difficult, and the sun had set before I found and shot the stag I was looking for. Deciding that it was too late to bring in the deer that night I covered it up to give it a measure of protection against leopard, bear and pig and made for home, intending to return with a carrying party early next morning.

My shot had been heard in the village and I found ten or a dozen men waiting for me on the steps of our cottage, equipped with ropes and a stout bamboo pole. In reply to their questions I told them I had shot the deer they wanted, and added that if they met me at the village gate at sunrise next morning I would take them to where I had covered it up. The men had come prepared to bring in the deer that night and they said that if I would tell them where the deer was they would go out and try

to find it for themselves. On the previous occasions on which I
had shot deer for the village, I had laid a trail. The men knew
the jungles as well as I did and all the information they needed,
when I shot meat for them, was the position of the mark I had
made on fire-track, game-path, or cattle-track, and from this
mark they would follow the trail I had laid. This system of
recovering an animal had never failed, but on the present occasion,
having shot the deer late in the evening and there being no moon,
I had not laid a trail. The men were anxious to divide up the
deer that night in preparation for the feast on the morrow, and
as I did not wish to disappoint them I told them to go up the
Powalgarh fire-track for two and a half miles and wait for me
at the foot of an old *haldu* tree that was a landmark known to
all of us. So while the men streamed out of the compound I sat
down to a cup of tea Maggie had brewed for me.

A man walking alone can cover the ground much faster than
a body of men walking in Indian file, so I did not hurry over
my tea, and when I picked up my rifle to follow the men it was
quite dark. I had walked a good few miles between sunrise and
sunset that day but being as fit as man could be an additional
five or six miles meant nothing to me. The men had a good
start but they were still some distance from the *haldu* tree when
I caught them up. I had no difficulty in finding the deer, and
when the men had lashed it to the bamboo pole I took them
back by a short cut which reduced the distance by half a mile.
It was dinner-time when I got back to our cottage, and telling
Maggie I would postpone my bath until bedtime, I asked her to
call for dinner while I had a wash.

When undressing to have my bath that night I was very
surprised to find that my light rubber-soled shoes were full of
red dust, and that my feet were coated with it. I am very careful
of my feet and have in consequence never suffered from any

form of foot trouble, and I could not understand how I had
been so careless as to get my feet all messed up. Small things
have a habit of nagging at the memory and the memory in turn
nags at the nerves that control the cells in which information
is stored, and then, suddenly and without any conscious effort
on our part the information we are seeking—be it the name of
a person, or of a place, or as in the present case the reason for
my messed-up feet—is presented to us.

The old trunk road which carried all the traffic to the hills
before the railway to Kathgodam was built, runs in a straight
line from our gate to the Boar bridge. Three hundred yards
beyond the bridge the road turns to the left. On the right-hand
side of this turn the road, at the time I am writing of, was met
by the Powalgarh fire-track which for a few hundred yards
followed the alignment of the present Powalgarh motor road.
Fifty yards from the Boar bridge the trunk road is met on the
right by the Kota road coming down from the north. Between
the junction of these two roads and the turn, the road runs
through a shallow depression. Heavy cart traffic had churned
up the red earth in the depression, resulting in the road at this
point being six inches deep in dust. To avoid walking in the dust
the foot traffic had trodden a narrow path between the dusty
road and the jungle on the left. Thirty yards on the near side
of the turn, the road and the narrow footpath ran over a small
culvert which had parapet walls a foot thick and eighteen inches
high, to prevent carts running off the road. The culvert had ceased
to function many years previously and at the lower end of it, i.e.
the end nearer the narrow footpath, there was a bed of sand
eight or ten feet square on a level with the road.

The information concerning my dirty feet that had been
brought back to memory was, that when following my men after

tea I had left the narrow footpath a few yards on the near side of the culvert; crossed the road from left to right through the six-inch-deep dust; skirted along the right-hand edge of the road and after passing over the culvert, recrossed the road, and continued along the footpath. Why had I done this? From the time I left our cottage, to the time I overtook the men near the *haldu* tree, I had not heard a single sound that had given me even the suspicion of uneasiness, and I had seen nothing, for it was a dark night. Why then had I crossed the road, and after passing over the culvert, recrossed it?

I have stated earlier in this book that from the day I traced the terrifying sound made by Dansay's banshee as the friction of two smooth surfaces, I have made a hobby of finding a reason for every unusual thing I have heard or seen in the jungles. Well, here was something unusual, something that needed an explanation, so before there was any traffic on the road next morning I went out to try to get the explanation.

The men after leaving our gate the previous evening had gone down the road in a bunch and had been joined at the village gate by an additional three men, bringing the number to fourteen. After crossing the Boar bridge the party had proceeded along the footpath in Indian file crossed the culvert, and at the turn crossed from the left to the right of the road, and gone up the fire-track. Shortly thereafter, a tiger came down the Kota road, scratched up the ground near a bush at the junction of the two roads, crossed the trunk road, and proceeded along the footpath. Here the tiger's pug marks were superimposed on the footprints of my men. When the tiger had proceeded along the footpath for about thirty yards, I came over the bridge.

The bridge is an iron one and quite evidently the tiger heard me crossing it, for I was walking fast and making no attempt to

go silently. When the tiger found I was not going up the Kota road, but was coming in his direction, he hurried down the footpath and, leaving it at the culvert, lay down on the patch of sand facing the road and with his head a yard from the footpath. I followed the tiger down the footpath and when I was within five yards of the culvert I turned to the right, crossed the road through the six-inch-deep dust, skirted along the right edge of the road, and after passing over the culvert recrossed the road to the footpath. And this I had done *unconsciously*, to avoid passing within a yard of the tiger.

I believe that if I had continued along the footpath I could have passed the tiger with perfect safety provided (*a*) that I had proceeded steadily on my way, (*b*) that I had made no vocal sound, (*c*) that I had made no violent movement. The tiger had no intention of killing me, but if at the moment of passing him I had stopped to listen to any jungle sound, or had coughed or sneezed or blown my nose, or had thrown the rifle from one shoulder to the other, there was a chance that the tiger would have got nervous and attacked me. My subconscious being was not prepared to take this risk and jungle sensitiveness came to my assistance and guided me away from the potential danger.

On how many occasions jungle sensitiveness has

enabled me to avoid dangers of one kind or another it is not possible for me to say, but from the fact that in all the years I have lived in the jungles I have only once come in actual contact with a wild animal is proof that some sense, call it jungle sensitiveness, or call it my Guardian Angel, has intervened at the critical moment to ensure my safety.